HOW TO SUCCEED

WHERE IT

DISCOVER:
- ▶ Three decisions to prepare you for success ▶ Four freedoms that accompany true success ▶ Four characteristic values of a successful person ▶ Three principles to help you manage your time

REALLY

COUNTS

DOUG SHERMAN &
WILLIAM HENDRICKS

NAVPRESS ®
A MINISTRY OF THE NAVIGATORS
P.O. BOX 6000, COLORADO SPRINGS, COLORADO 80934

The Navigators is an international Christian organization. Jesus Christ gave His followers the Great Commission to go and make disciples (Matthew 28:19). The aim of The Navigators is to help fulfill that commission by multiplying laborers for Christ in every nation.

NavPress is the publishing ministry of The Navigators. NavPress publications are tools to help Christians grow. Although publications alone cannot make disciples or change lives, they can help believers learn biblical discipleship, and apply what they learn to their lives and ministries.

© 1989 by Doug Sherman and William Hendricks
All rights reserved, including translation
Library of Congress Catalog Card Number:
  89-62749
ISBN 08910-95810

Printed in the United States of America

FOR A FREE CATALOG OF
NAVPRESS BOOKS & BIBLE STUDIES,
CALL TOLL FREE 800-366-7788 (USA)
or 1-416-499-4615 (CANADA)

Contents

Preface   7

Part One: What Is Success?
   1. I'll Know Success When I See It!   13
   2. Life, Liberty, and the Pursuit of Success   24
   3. Preachers and Prosperity   35

Part Two: True Success
   4. How to Succeed Where It Really Counts   53
   5. Three Steps to True Success   70

Part Three: A New Way of Life
New Freedoms   91
   6. The Freedom to Enjoy Life   93
   7. The Freedom to Balance Life   98
   8. The Freedom to Care About People   108
   9. The Freedom to Accept Yourself   112

New Values   117
   10. A Value on Integrity   119
   11. A Value on Character   125
   12. A Value on Relationships   130
   13. A Value on Serving God   143

New Ways of Making Decisions   151
14. Decisions About Integrity   154
15. Decisions About Your Schedule   162
16. Decisions About Your Money   171
17. Don't Stop Here!   178

Your Success Strategy: A Manual for Growth   181
Session 1   185
   Our culture's perspectives on success.
Session 2   190
   Two views of success that some Christians hold.
Session 3   197
   The Bible's view of success.
Session 4   205
   The new freedoms that come from a biblical view of success.
Session 5   210
   The new values that a biblical view of success promotes.
Session 6   219
   How a biblical view of success affects your decisions.

Evaluation Form   227
We Want to Hear from You!   228

Authors

Doug Sherman is the founder and president of Career Impact Ministries (CIM), a Christian organization that helps business and professional people integrate their faith into their careers.

After graduating from the Air Force Academy with a B.S. in engineering management, Doug served as an instructor in the Advanced Jet Training Program, a position he held until he left the Air Force to attend Dallas Theological Seminary, where he received a Th.M.

Doug and his wife, Jan, live in Woodbridge, Virginia, and have three children.

William Hendricks is a writer and consultant in communication development. He received a B.A. in English literature from Harvard University, an M.S. in mass communications from Boston University, and an M.A. from Dallas Theological Seminary. He is the former vice president of CIM.

Bill lives in Dallas, Texas, with his wife, Nancy, and their two daughters.

Other books by Doug Sherman and William Hendricks:

YOUR WORK MATTERS TO GOD (NavPress, 1987)

HOW TO BALANCE COMPETING TIME DEMANDS
(NavPress, 1989)

Preface

In the library of Career Impact Ministries (CIM) head-quarters, we have an entire shelf of books devoted to success. Michael Korda's *Success!* is there. So is Napoleon Hill's classic, *Think and Grow Rich*. Dennis Waitley, Og Mandino, Zig Ziglar, and John Molloy are represented, along with numerous biographies and "how-to" primers.

Anyone familiar with the business and career sections of a typical bookstore would quickly recognize this genre. It's obvious that we as Americans *want* success. We want it badly—so badly that many of us are paying enormous prices to get it.

Perhaps that's why we have another shelf in CIM's library that is gradually filling up with a different type of book—one that reveals a very dark side to our culture's infatuation with success. Douglas LaBier's *Modern Madness: The Emotional Fallout of Success* is perhaps the most precise and comprehensive. But others paint a similar picture that success—as it is currently defined in America—is not all it's cracked up to be.

However, whether you're a success-genre junkie or a

success-scarred basket case, the rabbit-like proliferation of both these sets of books and their messages illustrates the profound truth that *ideas have consequences*.

This book is also about success. It's also written with the knowledge that ideas have consequences, that behavior follows belief, that what you think has a direct (though often unrecognized) bearing on how you act. The more powerful an idea and the more timely its arrival, the more dynamic its impact on the way people live.

That's why it's so crucial that before we throw ourselves into a lifelong commitment to achieving success, we determine what "success" really is. How do we define it? What does it look like? Is our picture of success valid? Is our culture's perception of success valid?

This book deals with such fundamental questions from the standpoint of the Bible. We're well aware that for most people, the Bible seems about as relevant to the topic of success as a hymnbook. Others assume that the Bible stands opposed to any thought of ambition. And for a growing number of others, the Bible is used to proof-text a rather greedy, self-serving way of life. These people believe God is obligated to shower His material blessings on His people.

Needless to say, there's a need for clarity in regard to the issue of success and what the Bible has to say about it. We hope this book helps to bring such clarity to the issue.

DUAL AUTHORSHIP

As is our habit, we've written this book in the first person singular, even though we are both its authors. The voice you hear is Doug's. Most of this material has come from his ministry to business and professional people in both a consulting capacity and as a speaker. Doug has refined this material into a series of taped messages, from which much of the book is derived. Keep in mind, however, that this project is very much a shared experience.

Acknowledgments

Countless individuals from an amazing array of backgrounds have assisted us in bringing this book to completion. We'd like to specifically thank John Maisel, Terry Prindiville, Butch McCaslin, Rick Nutter, Bill Robertson, Frank and Cathy Tanana, Mike Reilly, Howard Hendricks, Ed Johnson, Rex Sanders, Larry and Ann Ivey, Bob Buford, Fred Smith Jr., Mike Chadwick, Bill Anderson, Wayne Hey, Dave Mayfield, Ray Blunt, Charlie Olcott, and Jean Taft.

We're also grateful to the entire NavPress team, led by John Eames, Bruce Nygren, Volney James, and Steve Eames. And as with our previous books, Karolynn Simmons has distinguished herself as our most valuable player for her consistently high performance at the word processor.

Finally, we wish to thank our families: Jan, Jason, Matthew, and Jennifer Sherman, and Nancy, Brittany, and Kristin Hendricks. Whatever success we have or will attain is clearly due in large measure to their invaluable partnership.

DOUG SHERMAN
WILLIAM HENDRICKS

PART ONE

What Is Success?

I'll Know Success When I See It!

Imagine the shock that a friend of mine once felt when he turned to the business section of the Sunday paper and found the front page—the entire front page—devoted to him, his company, and his career success! The headline deemed him an "empire builder," and the subtitle described him as a "tough, inventive tycoon." A color photo dominated the page and made him look every bit as impressive as he was supposed to be.

The article began by describing the office of my friend—I'll call him Peter. Peter's "desk has no chair—he works standing up. Employees of his company know that their thirty-six-year-old president's pursuit of productivity doesn't stop with himself. In fact, he recently installed an employees' cafeteria in the company's building because employees take less time for lunch when they eat in. And to clamp down on employees' use of office supplies and the telephone, he hired an 'enforcer' who, he said, saved the company $70,000 in one year."

The article went on to say that Peter's "shrewd and inventive ways are what make him one of the most powerful real estate tycoons in two counties. A local realtor says of him, 'He always comes up on top. He's in the position where he has a lot to say. I try to be better prepared when dealing with [Peter]. He's made a lot of wise investments. He knew what he was doing when he bought property. He's built an empire.'"

Suppose you were my friend Peter. Would you feel successful? If the paper says you are, would you *be* successful? The local realtor says you are; but what would *you* think?

HOW DO YOU DEFINE SUCCESS?

Most of us aren't philosophers. We don't usually sit around and consciously ask questions like: What do I really need to be happy and fulfilled in life? What achievement must I have to feel important? What would convince me that I've made a mark on human history?

Nevertheless, each of us has an idea of what success would mean for us, some mental image of what we'd look like if we achieved our fondest dreams.

When I was in college at the Air Force Academy, my picture of success was to start on the varsity football team. It was the thing I lived for and dreamed about. Every night I'd open my books and try to study; yet all I could think about was football, football, football! My success in life centered on starting on the team and playing football.

Later, when I became an officer, success would be the day I could pin three stars on my uniform. Lowly captain that I was, I set my ambitious sights on those shiny stars. (One star wouldn't be enough; I had to have three!) Success meant becoming a three-star general.

How about you? What does success mean for you?

If you're a man, success for you likely revolves around your career—the idea that you're holding down a responsible job that adequately provides for you and, if you're married, your family. Of course, many men aim far beyond keeping a steady job. Some want to become "peak performers"—valuable employees who are the best at what they do. Others make it their ambition to run the company. For some, like my friend Peter, that's still not enough: they intend to *own* the company.

Not that these ambitions are limited to men. For an increasing number of women, success in life is measured by success in one's career. This is by no means true of all working women (or men), nor is it the only factor that has brought millions of women into the work force in the last twenty years. But there are enough women like Sally Fields, Leona Helmsley, and Mary Kay Ash featured in *Ms.* and *Savvy* and *Working Woman* and *Lears* to paint a portrait of feminine success in distinctively careerist colors.

If you're a career homemaker—perhaps with every intention of remaining such—you may paint the picture much differently. For you, success may be connected to your husband and his performance on the job, his position, achievements, and income. Likewise, what becomes of your children matters a lot to your sense of accomplishment and satisfaction. Your family *is* your job, so their relative success in life has a direct bearing on yours.

Which brings us to the differing perceptions of success between parents and children. What would your kids have to do for you to regard them as successful? That's not a question parents get asked every day, but I guarantee you answer it every day, especially for your kids.

For instance, I occasionally hear a father say, "All I care about is that my child does his best!" That sounds good, pretty reasonable and healthy. But that may not be what the father communicates to his son or daughter. If you asked the child to describe success, and if you could get a straightforward answer, he would likely frame his picture of success in terms of pleasing his parents, especially his dad. After all, where did his father pick up his own notions of success and failure? No doubt out of the dynamics between himself and his own father. He then passes on that legacy to his own children.

HOW DO YOU MEASURE SUCCESS?

I find that for most of us, the only thing harder than defining success is achieving it. We have a hard time pinning down exactly what it is—but we know it when we see it. Perhaps that's why each occupation and profession relies on certain symbols that signify success, little badges of honor exhibited by those who have "arrived."

I mentioned the tremendous significance that three stars held for me as a captain in the Air Force. Likewise, many a young lawyer aims at becoming a partner in a law firm, and having his name added to the shingle. Salespeople are forever striving to win plaques and trophies that mark them as excelling above their peers. In Washington, D.C., influence is everything, so government workers and politicians prefer pictures of themselves with the President, preferably signed by the latter, to show off their proximity to power.

Bill once showed me an intriguing article about a young man who never felt successful until he purchased a $1,000 suit. Imagine that! He said he felt a bolt of self-confidence whenever he put that suit on! It made him feel adequate to get ahead. He swore there was something magical about the $1,000 price tag.

In sports, every athlete dreams of championship trophies. A reporter once praised a former Dallas Cowboys running back for his outstanding performance. In response, the superstar brandished a beefy fist crowned by his massive Super Bowl ring and declared, "Without the ring, it don't mean a thing!" Similarly in television advertising, the Clio awards distinguish the masterpieces from the mundane. Film industry entertainers seek Oscars. Journalists pursue Pulitzers. Recording artists croon for Grammys.

In corporations, dozens of little signals help the players keep score. What's your title? Where is your office? How does the president or CEO address you? *Does* he address you? Where do you sit at company banquets? Has your name appeared in *Forbes*, *Business Week*, or *The Wall Street Journal*? In what light? Are you a frequent flyer on the company plane? Are you a regular in the company's suite at the stadium, or do you own your own suite?

All across the wide world of work, evaluating success inevitably results in keeping score. This leads us to questions such as: Who keeps score? Who determines when you're a success? Who measures the shadow you cast? You alone? Your boss? Your employees? Your customers? For that matter, how do your peers regard your status? Would your parents evaluate you as a successful person? What if the media wrote you up, as happened with my friend Peter? Are they the ultimate referees of who has "made it"? Or are they merely showcasing celebrities for a bored public? Is there some primeval, societal intuition about who is successful and who is not?

THE ENGINE OF SUCCESS

Success is hard to measure, even harder to define. Yet it seems everyone wants to succeed. I know I do, and I suspect you do, as well. My guess is that you've picked up this book to help you achieve that goal. And I want to help you if I can.

For the past ten years, I've made a personal study of the powerful urge we all seem to have to excel, to achieve, to become the person of our dreams. I've talked with some of the most successful men and women in our society, as well as hundreds still climbing to the top. Some have been successful and satisfied; others successful and miserable. Some have had a deep, genuine, religious faith and commitment; others have been profoundly secular and skeptical of the relevance of religion. Some have pursued carefully crafted strategies to get where they are, others have stumbled onto success.

Although each of them defines, describes, or illustrates success a bit differently, they have a number of things in common with the rest of us. For example, they show us that how we define and measure success is probably one of the most important things about us. It's like a mighty engine that pulls our life along.

Think how important our image of success is. It determines what we think about, what we dream about, what we worry about, and how we spend our time. It has an awful lot to do with how we spend our money. Our image of success tells a lot about our character and of what kind of metal we're made.

In fact, our picture of success profoundly affects our self-worth. For example, if we believe that having money will make us successful but we don't have a lot of money, then we'll likely feel insignificant. If we define success in terms of mental abilities but didn't get into Harvard, then we may have lingering doubts about our intelligence. If owning a business is our ticket to success but we've lost millions on one failed venture after another, we'll likely question our worth as a person.

This brings us to a further observation: Our definition of success determines the priorities in our lives. Recall how football became my highest priority during my first year at the Academy. It was all I could think about. In the business and professional world, I've known men and women who have sacrificed marriages, families, friendships, even morals if necessary, in pursuit of the shining vision of success. As Ray Kroc of McDonald's hamburgers fame put it: he believed in God, family, and McDonald's—but in the office that order was reversed! Or consider Herbert von Karajan, world-renowned conductor of the Berlin Philharmonic. In younger days he declared that he would sacrifice his grandmother, if necessary, to fulfill his musical "mission." After World War II he explained away his membership in the Nazi Party as merely an opportunistic career move.

WHY THIS BOOK?

Success is a powerful force, at times almost godlike in its control over our lives. As such, it deserves careful consideration before we hand ourselves over to do its bidding. That's why Bill and I wrote this book.

As we surveyed the endless stream of success-related materials flooding the marketplace recently, we felt strongly that one resource had yet to be produced. Not just another "how-to" pitch; there are enough of those! But a much more fundamental message, a book that deals with a far more important issue: *What is real* success? Is it something that each person determines for himself? Or is there a "true success" that anyone can understand and pursue with all his heart? We think there is, and that's what this book is about.

We want to challenge the picture of success painted by our culture—especially when defined exclusively in terms of career success. As you'll see, there's nothing inherently wrong with career success. But there's everything wrong with equating success in life to success on the job. If you're driven and ambitious, willing to do whatever it takes to climb to the top of the pile, you'll not want to skip the next chapter. You may discover that you've been scaling the wrong mountain!

On the other hand, you may already feel like a winner in your career but a loser everywhere else. You may be like the man who contacted an acquaintance of Bill's and announced: "I own my own firm. I personally netted two million dollars last year. I expect to make twice that this year. My wife and kids won't speak to me. I'm living out of a hotel room. What's wrong?" If you've tasted sweet victory only to have it turn bitter and sickening, I hope you'll find encouragement and hope in the following pages.

What about the person who feels tension between faith and work? You may struggle because your career encourages your best efforts and rewards you accordingly, yet the teaching of your faith sometimes appears to contradict that drive, appealing instead for self-renunciation and the forsaking of worldly success. This creates a real problem, because you want to please God with your life; but you also want to achieve great things in your career using your God-given abilities. At times, you may wonder, "Isn't there any way to please God *and* succeed in life?" We'll look closely at this issue in chapter

2. It's unfortunate that a faulty view of work widely taught among Christians today creates this needless tension.

In part two, we'll examine what "true success" is, as defined by God. You may be surprised by the idea of bringing God into a discussion about success, particularly career success. But, as we'll see, a successful life and career have everything to do with living life as He intended.

WHAT'S IN IT FOR YOU?

Pursuing that true success leads to a number of valuable benefits. We'll look at many of them in detail in part three. But based on the experiences of many who have studied this material before, I can summarize several benefits that you can expect:

Understanding What Real Success Is All About

As I've already indicated, there's a lot of confusion today over how to define and measure success. Fortunately, we can look to God for insight and perspective. His definition of success cuts through the fog of shifting cultural values and brings us to the heart of what success is all about.

Relating Your Faith to Everyday Career Issues and Decisions

Most people, even many Christians, assume that religion has nothing to contribute to the workplace. But when they discover how much God cares about their day-to-day work issues and how much He has to say about them, they find a dramatic new interest in applying God's truth to the situations they face on the job each day.

Freedom from Guilt

So many of us stagger under a load of guilt, sensing that despite our best efforts, we're not pleasing God with our lives. The issue of success lies at the heart of the problem: We want to succeed but feel that God wouldn't want us to. However, when we redefine success from God's perspective, it offers us a new way to do our best in life *and* please God. The result is a release from guilt and a refreshing sense of God's approval.

Freedom from Crushing Expectations

Success can become a harsh taskmaster. Those driven by it serve endless demands of performance and image. But adopting a godly view of success unburdens us of unhealthy expectations and introduces us instead to a refreshing sense of freedom that was impossible before.

New Values That Put Life and Work into Proper Perspective

Understanding what real success is helps you sort out the big fish in life from the little fish—the things that really matter from the things that are trivial. You'll be able to concentrate on catching the big fish—and letting the little ones go.

A New Way of Making Decisions

For many people, career success makes all their decisions. It drives their choices about time, money, and the use of emotional energy. But a godly view of success transforms this decision-making process, introducing the freedom to choose what is right and healthy rather than what is expedient.

In short, this book introduces more than just a few new concepts or "how-to" strategies. It presents a whole new way of living, thinking, and working. It's not intended to help you make money or become the CEO of your corporation or get yourself written up in the paper. Nothing wrong with those; but this book aims at something much more significant: to help you be a success where it really counts—before God! That's the one arena in which you absolutely don't want to fail.

Of course, the place to start our discussion is with success as it's defined on the street. Everyone wants to succeed in life; and our culture has definite ideas about what success looks like. I invite you to begin in the next chapter by looking at the picture painted by the career world.

CHAPTER TWO

Life, Liberty, and the Pursuit of Success

Have you ever noticed how so many things in life depend on an understanding of unspoken assumptions? The following true story illustrates how important such assumptions can be.

A young graduate student facing graduation had started to look for his first "real" job. His inquiries landed him an interview with an executive search firm. Attired in a new suit and clutching his modest resumé, he arrived at his appointment five minutes early. The receptionist asked him to have a seat and buzzed the recruiter's secretary. A woman emerged from a hallway and invited him to follow her.

They went to a small office where a portly gentleman in shirtsleeves rose from behind a desk and extended a powerful handshake. The interview began.

"Tell me about yourself," opened the recruiter.

"Well, let me show you my resumé," responded the youth, handing over a neatly typed two-page document. He reviewed the highlights of his accomplishments to date, while the eyes of the examiner scanned the pages for a few brief moments.

Then the recruiter dropped the papers on his desk and looked into the eyes of his nervous prospect. "So what sort of position are you looking for?"

"Well," began the student, "as you can see, my background is in marketing, though I've had some experience in teaching. I'd really like to find something in training, perhaps sales training. I really enjoy teaching people how to do things."

The interviewer paused and then threw him a curve ball: "What sort of work does your father do?"

Trying hard to disguise his surprise, the young man explained, "He's a teacher. He teaches high school biology."

"Have you ever had any experience with a large company?" queried the interviewer, barely waiting for him to finish.

"Well, as you'll notice on my resumé, I worked on a publicity project with the American Cancer Society."

"I think that was a school project, wasn't it?" The boy replied that it was. "But I mean, you've never done an internship with a Fortune 500 company?"

"No, sir."

"Do any of your friends have fathers who work in the corporate world?" The student thought for a moment, and then nodded. "Well, let me advise you to get with some of those men and ask them what big business is all about."

At this the young prospect shifted nervously and began to ask why, when the recruiter cut him off. "I don't really think you understand what you're getting into. There's a whole culture to the business world that I'm not sure you're familiar with. It has its own set of rules, its own look, even its own language. It asks certain kinds of questions, and it's looking for a certain kind of person who will fit in. You don't strike me as that sort of person."

Feeling rejected before his interview was barely five minutes old, the student began to protest, arguing that he was an intelligent individual and all he needed was a chance to prove himself. The recruiter agreed, but encouraged him to take his advice and meet with men employed in the corporate world. "And then maybe we can talk," he said, standing up to bring the interview to a close.

UNSPOKEN ASSUMPTIONS

Professionals in the field of career placement could point out many flaws in the graduate student's approach. On the surface they might fault him for wearing the wrong suit, or having the wrong haircut, or maybe even having a beard. They might tell him to get his resumé typeset and to bring it in a dark leather briefcase.

More fundamentally, they might counsel him early in his studies to get experience as an intern with a major corporation, to start building his rolodex of corporate contacts, and to narrow down his search for employment to a specific type of job or career track in one certain company. They also could show him how to do research on the firm before going to the interview.

In short, veterans of the job search might have saved this student a lot of trouble by introducing him ahead of time to some of the many unspoken assumptions that people in corporate life share. That was the essence of the recruiter's suggestion about speaking with men in the business world. Such men would introduce him to the rules of the game.

At least they might have tried. The problem with trying to explain unspoken assumptions is that for every rule there are a dozen exceptions. Exceptions or not, however, that doesn't stop people from trying to play according to the rules—or from being penalized when they break them.

SUCCESS BY DEFAULT

Just as there are a number of unspoken assumptions that make the corporate arena what it is, there are a host of unspoken assumptions in the broader world of work that define what success is all about. As I pointed out in chapter 1, we don't always consciously think about what it means to be a success. Yet we tend to function from a mental picture of what success would look like if we were to achieve it.

What's interesting is how similar that picture looks for most of us. It's like a computer program that has a set of defaults in it. A word-processing program, for instance, comes from the manufacturer with a number of preset parameters. The margins are set for so many spaces of indentation, the font is set for a certain popular typeface, the characters are set to be a certain size, and so on. Unless you override the program, the program will always default back to those original values.

In a similar way, when it comes to success most of us tend to default to a common set of values. It's a set of unspoken but powerful assumptions that our culture—particularly the career world—has given us. Unless we override the program and adjust the parameters of success, by default we'll tend to pursue success as our culture defines it.

What are those unspoken assumptions about success? Let me mention four. First, to be successful you have to have *money*. To be happy and to feel fulfilled and important, you must have money. Without it you are nothing. Money is how we keep score. Michael Korda in his best-selling book *Success!* said "It's just as well to face it squarely, the successful get rich, and the unsuccessful get poor." He went on to argue that wealth is a powerful motivator: "The simple ambition to live better is a potent factor in succeeding. What you have now has to be intolerable compared to what you want."[1] In other words, success is always wanting more.

A second default in the success program is *professional recognition*. To be a success, your accomplishments must overwhelm your contemporaries. To be only average is a failure; to be below average is a disastrous failure.

Pamela Pettler in a little book called *The Joy of Stress*, offered a satirical essay on the anxieties surrounding professional recognition. In a section entitled, "They're Getting Ahead of You," she wrote:

> One day in late 1969, in the research library of the University of California in Berkeley, a young man went berserk. He ran through the library, shouting hysterically at his astonished fellow students, "Stop! Stop! You're getting ahead of me!"
>
> He was arrested. But what was his crime, really? *Being in the wrong decade.* As we all know, the sixties era, and its childish preoccupation with peace, good sex, and battered VW buses, was little more than a black mark, a shameful demerit in the History of Stress.
>
> Now, of course, in the stress-filled eighties, this concept of "getting ahead of me" has regained

its rightful place of importance. In fact, it is one of the basic precepts of stress.

Simply stated, *people are getting ahead of you.* All the time.

While you're at your desk, people working out at the gym are getting ahead of you.

While you're at the gym, your co-workers are getting ahead of you.

If a friend gets a promotion at work, she has gotten ahead of you.

If a colleague reads a book you haven't read, he has gotten ahead of you.

The entire U.S. swim team has gotten ahead of you.

While you're reading this book, *everyone* is getting ahead of you.

The beauty of the concept is that it can be applied across the board, anywhere, anytime.

On the road? Drivers of more expensive cars have gotten ahead of you.

Watching TV? All the writers, actors, and technical crews have gotten ahead of you.

At Marine World? The *dolphins* have gotten ahead of you.

Always judge yourself, and your intrinsic moral worth, in terms of specific achievements as compared to others.[2]

Along with money and professional recognition, there's another parameter of success: *power*, especially the power to control other people. People who have it are successful. People without it aren't worth bothering with.

As I've mentioned, Washington, D.C., is a city built

on influence. A recent piece in the *Wall Street Journal* poked fun at how this phenomenon of power operates on the D.C. party circuit. As the Reagan administration stepped down and the Bush administration stepped forward, the stock of various party-going Washingtonians fell or rose accordingly, the article pointed out. Incoming Commerce Secretary Robert Mosbacher and his wife, Georgette, had suddenly become in-demand as preferred guests. On the other hand, interest in columnist George Will—who had been a frequent luncheon partner to Nancy Reagan—was in decline.

The business world operates in a similar fashion. One can hear it in an old saying about finance: "The men who manage men manage the men who manage things, but the men who manage money manage the men who manage men."

To money, professional recognition, and power I might add what I call *"the four Cs."* The four Cs are closet space, cars, clubs, and clothes. A person who has a large house (closet space) in the right neighborhood is considered successful. As for one's car, it's not just the size that matters any more; now it's what country the car comes from! Likewise, the prestige of one's dining and country clubs is important. And of course, the cut and color of one's suit or dress tells everyone whether or not he or she is "dressed for success."

Money. Status. Power. The four Cs. Doubtless there are many other elements to the unwritten rules of success. But you get the picture. To have any one of these is to have success. To have all four is to be wildly successful! Men and women all across our nation are pursuing that dream—a vision in which success in life equals success in one's career. They never intend to end up as alcoholics or to have their kids on drugs or to detonate their marriages. On the contrary, they hope to end up on top of life as winners. And there's nothing wrong with that.

However, let's make some observations that challenge this common perception of success. First, notice how the career world almost always defines success in quantitative, not qualitative terms.

A man might be an alcoholic, he might be on his second, third or even fourth marriage, his kids might be on drugs, his associates might hate his guts—but if he's filthy rich, the CEO of a big company, dines regularly with Senators and Congressmen, or flies to his vacation house in Vail in his private plane, what do we call him? A success!

On the other hand, have you ever been to a banquet where someone was honored for a great marriage? Or for spending time with his kids? Or for honesty and integrity? Probably not! Banquets usually honor someone for achievements and performance, such as being tops in sales. Success in the business and professional world is quantitative, not qualitative.

A second observation is that success in life is reached almost exclusively through career achievement. It's as if nothing else matters besides work; certainly nothing matters as much as work.

One of the most perceptive observers of this tendency is psychologist Douglas LaBier of Washington, D.C. In his excellent book *Modern Madness*, he documents the fact that careerism has become the main work ethic of our times. Careerism, he says, "is an attitude, a life orientation in which a person views career as the primary and most important aim of life."[3]

Consequently, the career becomes sacred. Marriage, children, friendships, and morals if necessary, must accommodate themselves to career demands or else be left behind. As LaBier points out in chilling terms, this opens up a dark side to success that few people perceive when they first take off down their "career path."

Which brings us to a third observation: The bright and shining vision of success that seems to drive so many people tends to promise more than it delivers. The road to the top is littered with the wreckage of lives broken by the rat race. For every "winner" featured in a slick magazine article, there are countless "losers" quietly eliminated by needless burnout, debilitating addictions of all kinds, disastrous business ventures, and even criminal convictions.

However, life at the top is not as rich and creamy as it's served up in print. Success stories make for great reading, probably because they reinforce the images we all dream about. But beyond the reach of the press and the cameras is the reality that no amount of money, fame, position, or power can satisfy a person's deepest needs. Jesus Christ already warned us of this when He asked what profit there is in gaining the whole world but losing one's soul (see Matthew 16:24-26).

How can this be? Why do those who "have it all" so often report feeling empty and lifeless? Perhaps because of a fourth observation: The image of success promoted by our society doesn't just say it's okay to have money, professional recognition, power, and a lifestyle of comfort and convenience; it says you *need* them. Without them, you will live an insignificant, impoverished, unfulfilled life.

It is this burning need to succeed that corrupts human ambition, turning it into greed and selfishness. Granted, it may at times drive us to do better work; but does it ever make us better people?

If you *must* succeed—as the world defines success—if you're driven by ambition and compelled to reach the top, then you might as well face the fact that success is your god. If your career so dominates your life that it defines your self-worth, becomes the controlling center of your life, and is by far first among all your priorities, then you have made an idol of career success.

Which brings us to one final observation: When it comes to defining success, most people leave God out of the equation. They assume He doesn't belong in a discussion of success. It's not that they feel particularly negative toward religion, though many do. It's just assumed that matters of faith are irrelevant at that point. To even suggest that God might have something to say about success is, for many people, to commit an impropriety. Bring up God's perspective in a discussion on someone's success and watch the raised eyebrows and the glances that seem to ask, "Who invited you?"

At this point the popular image of success is exposed as a fraud. For if you leave God out of your view of success, success will become your god. It's that simple. We were created to enjoy life as God's companions and coworkers, which has enormous bearing on what true success is all about. If we define success apart from God, we cut ourselves off from the Source of our life. We adopt a lie, a counterfeit picture of success that ultimately leads to sorrow, not satisfaction.

We'll examine what God says about success in more detail in chapters 4 and 5. For now, let me challenge you—even if you consider yourself to be a strong Christian with a solid commitment to biblical truth. If you've been pursuing a vision of success in which you end up with money to buy what you want, or acclaim from your peers to bolster your feelings of worth, or power to control your world, or a lifestyle of comfort and convenience—if these are the kinds of things you picture when you think of success, if these are what motivate you to get up each day and head to your job, if these are things you think about, dream about, read about, and even pray for—then you may be far down the road toward personal and spiritual ruin! I'll explain why when we get to chapter 4.

First, we need to address a misconception about God and success. Some people have the idea that God Himself is opposed to success. They talk as if He were offended by or afraid of wealth, recognition, power, or luxury, as if these were inherently evil. Is that what God says? Read the next chapter and find out.

NOTES 1. Michael Korda, *Success!* (New York: Random House, 1977), pages 66-67.
2. Pamela Pettler, *The Joy of Stress* (New York: Quill, 1984), pages 22-25.
3. Douglas LaBier, *Modern Madness* (Reading, Mass.: Addison-Wesley Publishing Company, Inc., 1986), page 25.

CHAPTER THREE

Preachers and Prosperity

Have you ever read a book or heard a sermon, tape, or seminar that addressed practical workday issues from a biblical perspective? If so, you should consider yourself unusually fortunate, because based on research my organization has done, more than ninety percent of people who attend church never have.

It's as if God had nothing to say on the subject—which is exactly what most people conclude. What's worse, in the rare instances when church-goers do hear the subject of work addressed from the pulpit, it's usually in disparaging and/or uninformed terms. Here is a sample of what I'm talking about.

THE PASTOR'S PERSPECTIVE

Allen operated a landscape architecture firm. He started the business in his thirties, and for more than eleven years added some impressive projects to his portfolio. Some of his designs had won honors from prestigious professional associations.

Through those years, Allen's wife, Joy, had been extremely supportive in this venture. While he paid his dues to build his business, she bore the lion's share of child-raising responsibilities. The couple enjoyed their marriage, and their children appeared to be normal, healthy teenagers.

But the economy in Allen's area turned bad. Real estate development came to a standstill, which meant that no one needed landscape designs. The impact on Allen's firm was devastating. Most of the architects he didn't layoff began to leave for more prosperous regions.

One day Allen took stock of his situation and figured he could hold on for about one more year, maybe two with luck. But forecasts indicated that the economy wouldn't begin to turn around for at least that long. And even if it did, his firm's services would not be needed until six months into a recovery.

Discouraged, he discussed the situation with Joy. She suggested that he really seek God's perspective on the matter.

"But who can I talk to?" he asked.

"Why not Pastor Thompson?" she replied.

Allen shook his head. "Jim doesn't know the first thing about running a landscape architecture firm!"

"No," responded Joy, "but he sure seems to know God. That ought to count for something."

"You're right. I guess it can't hurt."

So Allen went to see the pastor one day after work.

After the two men exchanged pleasantries, Allen laid out his situation, and the pastor listened patiently. Finally, Allen concluded by summarizing his options.

"I've considered relocating, like some of the guys who used to work for me. But Joy and the kids are so happy here. Somehow I feel a . . . well, a responsibility,

I guess, to this community, to ride things out, to do my part for the prosperity of this town. I mean, I still employ a few people. No sense throwing them out of work."

Pastor Thompson smiled and slowly nodded.

"Then again," Allen continued, "I've also considered cutting my losses, laying low, and then jumping back in when things pick up. There's no point in jeopardizing my family's welfare just to keep up a shingle. There are jobs I could do just for the cash flow. And I think my staff could probably find work elsewhere— maybe even better work!"

Allen noticed that the pastor was chewing on his lip, obviously in intense thought. But since he said nothing, Allen continued.

"Of course, if I really wanted to go for it, I could probably swing a bridge loan. I don't have much collateral, but I've got enough equity in the firm to cover it, I think. Anyway, Joe—the commercial loan guy over at First—is a good friend of mine. You know Joe, don't you?"

The pastor shrugged. "I know who he is. He comes to church every few months. Can't say we're close."

"Well, I think he could vouch for me. At any rate, those are my options as I see them. There are others, but those are the three I'd seriously consider. My question is, Jim, is there any way to tell which one of those God thinks is best? I mean, this is my business on the line. Joy and I felt like we'd better really seek out God's will on this one. What do you think?"

Pastor Thompson leaned back in his chair and glanced out his window. Then he turned his head and looked Allen in the eye.

"Allen, I think God has brought you to a crossroads," he said grimly. Allen nodded slowly. "I think the hard times hitting this area right now are God's way of helping all of us come to see what is really important."

"Yeah, I guess when things are rolling along, it's easy to lose sight of all our blessings."

"Oh, it goes far beyond that. I think God's fed up with the emphasis this community has placed on money! I think He wants to win back His rightful place."

Allen pondered these words for a moment. "Are you saying that business is, well, sort of a god?"

"That's exactly right!"

"That sounds kind of strong."

"Allen, don't you see that business can be a distraction from what really matters?"

"I guess, but I always felt that business is a way to provide for your family."

"But that's my point! It's not business that provides for your family—it's God! 'My God shall supply all your needs,' Paul said. I think this city's dependence on its economy has become idolatry—and I think God is starting to show that to people."

Allen sat with his arms folded, contemplating the pastor's statements. Finally he asked, "Can you explain that a little bit more?"

"God never intended for us to rely on an income to meet our needs—only on Him. That's why every Sunday, in the Lord's Prayer, we ask, 'Give us this day our daily bread.' We're asking God for the bread. Jesus didn't tell us to pray, 'Give us this day a new contract, or a big commission, or a stock dividend.' In fact, Jesus told us clearly, 'Work not for the food which perishes, but for the food which remains unto eternal life.'"

"Yeah, but aren't we supposed to hold down a job to sort of help God provide that bread?"

"Yes, but in doing so you have to remember, 'Ye

cannot serve God and Mammon,' and realize that God doesn't need help to provide for your needs. That's something people need to learn from this downturn."

"Well, then, why do I work?" Allen asked, frustrated.

"A good question! The answer goes back to Genesis. Originally God gave man a perfect world in which his work was effortless. But when Adam and Eve sinned, God placed a curse on the world. One of the results was that work became toilsome and really a burden: 'By the sweat of your brow you shall eat bread.' Today we have to work because of sin. Of course, we'll be free from that curse in Heaven."

Allen reflected for a moment. "I guess I've always wondered about that. It seems like a hard truth to swallow. In fact, I can think of people in business who would never buy that. Work for them is, well, it's something they thrive on. A lot of guys feel that way. Our church doesn't have too many businessmen, but look at Tenth Avenue. From what I hear, they've got busloads coming every Sunday. Some big guns in the business community, too."

"Many churches preach a weaker Christianity," Pastor Thompson said. "It could be that they take their cues from the inherent greed and competition that drive our economy. They preach a soft message that could be boiled down to live a basically moral life, give a lot of money to the church, and God will take care of you. That kind of message is attractive, but it's empty. Too soft. I don't think God would ever honor it. Ecclesiastes calls that kind of life 'vanity'—futility!"

Allen shook his head. "If what you say is true, then I've spent the last eleven years of my life for nothing!"

Pastor Thompson smiled. "Allen, think about what

really matters. The only significant things are the things that will go on into eternity—people, God's work, God's Word. That's where we should put our time. On the things that last!"

"Not on moving dirt around in a landscape?" Allen asked wryly.

"It'll all burn up!" the pastor replied.

"So what are you saying I should do, Jim—quit my business and go into the ministry?"

"Only if God calls you. If He does, don't forsake that call. Don't be a Jonah! Of course, it's more likely that he wants you to be a layman."

"Yeah, I don't know whether I'm quite ready to become a missionary," Allen laughed.

"Maybe not. But have I helped answer some of your questions?"

Allen thought for a moment. "Not really—but you've sure given me a lot to think about!"

THE TWO-STORY VIEW OF WORK

Allen's situation is very real and not uncommon, although the pastor's statements are a composite of comments from many ministers. Perhaps you've heard remarks like his in sermons or read them in books. Bill and I have heard them countless times in a variety of settings. Taken together, they form a picture that actually misrepresents what God has said about work.

The pastor is promoting what I call a Two-Story view of work. Bill and I discuss this flawed teaching and its tragic implications in our book *Your Work Matters to God* (NavPress, 1987). I strongly encourage you to read that material, because it explains the problems with this view of work in greater detail.

The essence of the Two-Story view is that it divides life into two spheres, the "sacred" and the "secular." "Sacred" activities would obviously include religion and activities of faith and ritual—anything having to do with the spiritual side of life. "Secular" activities would involve whatever's left. Certainly everyday work would be considered secular, something that is not concerned with God and something with which God has no concern.

Of course that immediately leads to a hierarchy in which sacred things have more value than secular ones. After all, don't you want to give your life to what really counts—to *God*? Of course you do! But the Two-Story view says that what counts are things like Bible reading, prayer, worship, sermons, and charity. When it comes to vocations, what counts are the "full-time" ministries— the pastorate, missionary work, evangelism, and the like.

Where does that leave you if you're a landscape architect like Allen? Or a real estate developer like my friend Peter? Or a plumber? Or a computer salesperson? Or a career homemaker? Or any of the thousands of other "secular" occupations? The Two-Story view says your work in those jobs doesn't exactly count for God. It's only when you leave work and participate in religious activities or church work that you're doing anything significant for Him.

In fact, when it comes to the matter of success, the Two-Story view unloads with both barrels. It points out that God is utterly opposed to ambition, and we all know, don't we, that the secular work world is based on greed and ambition?

Various Bible verses are rehearsed to bolster this line of thought: "Do not work for the food which perishes, but for the food which endures to eternal life" (John 6:27); "Heaven and earth will pass away, but My words shall not pass away" (Matthew 24:35); "The rich man in the midst of his pursuits will fade away" (James 1:11). Or as Jesus told the rich young ruler, "Go and sell your possessions and give to the poor, and you shall have treasure in heaven; and come, follow Me" (Matthew 19:21). Consider that "God is opposed to the proud, but gives grace to the humble" (James 4:6, 1 Peter 5:5). On and on.

The bottom line of the Two-Story view is that your work in a secular job has no dignity or value before God. And if you go so far as to pay unusual attention to what you do—apply yourself, strive for excellence, and start achieving impressive career accomplishments and enjoying the resulting money, acclaim, position and other "trappings" of success—then according to this widely held view, you have forsaken God's will and sold out to a godless, evil, secular world.

That's what the Two-Story view teaches. Is that what the whole of the Bible teaches? No. I'm aware of how prevalent this sort of thinking is in Christian circles; and I'm familiar with the precedents for it in Church history. But it's wrong. It's a distortion of biblical truth.

YOUR WORK MATTERS TO GOD

The truth is that your work—your "secular" work—*does* matter to God. He places enormous value on what you do in your job, and He takes a keen interest in what happens in the workplace.

If you look at the overall teaching of Scripture on work, you'll find that work has *intrinsic* value to God because He Himself is a worker. (See, for example,

Genesis 1–2; Deuteronomy 11:1-7; Psalms 104, 111; John 4:34; Colossians 1:16-17.) He has created us in His image to be His coworkers (see Genesis 1:26-29, 2:8-15; Psalm 8). Work is not a curse, but a gift from God (Ecclessiastes 5:18-19).

Furthermore, work has *instrumental* value in that it accomplishes at least five broad purposes. According to the Bible: (1) through work we serve other people and meet their needs (Matthew 22:39, 1 Thessalonians 4:9-12); (2) through work we meet our own needs (2 Thessalonians 3:6-15); (3) through work we meet the needs of our families (1 Timothy 5:8); (4) through work we earn money to aid the poor and to further the spread of the gospel (Galatians 6:6, Ephesians 4:28); and (5) through work we have a practical means to express love for God (Matthew 22:37-38; Colossians 3:17,23-24).

Your work matters to God! He cares about your job and how you do it. He also cares about you as a worker. Which means that He's quite interested your success on the job, and what that means, and how it's attained. But before we examine in detail a biblical view of success, it's crucial to start with a biblical view of work.

Don't let anyone ever sell you a Two-Story view of life. It's as misguided as the secular image of success we looked at in chapter 2. The secular view assumes that God is irrelevant when it comes to career achievement and success. By contrast, the Two-Story view assumes that everyday work is fairly irrelevant to God. Neither view is accurate.

However, before looking at a true, biblical perspective on success, it's worth mentioning one other misconception that some Christians hold. It's a marriage between the popular image of success we looked at before and popular religion. It's called Prosperity Theology.

PROSPERITY THEOLOGY

I once traveled to Budapest, Hungary. As I drove down one of the central boulevards in the city, I thought how nice the buildings looked—they were absolutely beautiful. They looked as captivating and impressive as any buildings in any city I'd ever been in. After traversing the main thoroughfare for several blocks, I turned down a side street. Then, I noticed the reality behind those beautiful buildings: many were merely facades. On the back they were completely crumbled, just worthless ruins. Only the fronts had been maintained to impress unsuspecting visitors on the main street.

Prosperity Theology is very similar to those buildings in Budapest. It looks great on the outside; but when you look a little closer, you find that it has absolutely no depth, nothing you'd really want to build your life on. It's a facade, masquerading as God's truth.

It goes by different names, depending on the part of the country you live in and who you're talking to. Some people call it a "health-and-wealth gospel," others refer to it as the "name-it-and-claim-it teaching," still others say "faith formula theology." I prefer the name Prosperity Theology. We can summarize the main ideas of this view as follows.

First, it holds that God wants His children (Christians) to prosper, especially in terms of material wealth. It's not that God says it's just okay to prosper—He says that His children *will* prosper, indeed they *must* prosper.

Furthermore, this view teaches that the Bible promises, literally guarantees, a path toward success and prosperity. If we'll follow certain formulas of faith and financial giving, then God will rain the treasures of Heaven down upon our heads. We'll be abundantly blessed. We'll succeed as we've never succeeded before.

If one is not prosperous, then to those with this view, that indicates sin or a lack of faith. Somehow that person has missed the magical formula that brings God's prosperity. Perhaps he's under Satan's control. Perhaps God is testing him. Certainly he's not prospering!

Perhaps you're familiar with ideas like these. I hope you haven't bought into them! In my opinion this sort of teaching is an insidious heresy tailor-made for our success-driven culture. Its appeal is very slick: Do you want a fancy car? Are you trying to get it through merely human effort? Why don't you let God get you that car by claiming a specific verse, then by visualizing God giving you that car? He wants you to have it, you know. He wants His children to enjoy the good things in life: If Christians were poor and miserable, who would want to be one? Besides, He is God, so He can do it. He wants to do it. Would God want His child to ride around in an old clunker? No, if He could take old Elijah home in a fiery chariot, He can certainly call up a new car for you!

In this way, Prosperity Theology panders to the greed of people, elevating it to a virtue through its use of Bible verses and the trappings of religion. Even worse, this is in direct contradiction to Jesus' warning:

> "Beware, and be on your guard against every form of greed; for not even when one has an abundance does his life consist of his possessions." (Luke 12:15)

I won't refute Prosperity Theology in detail. But here are a few points to consider.

God never guarantees financial prosperity or health to Christians in the New Testament. The Lord Jesus, as you know, was a man born into humble circumstances. He had few clothes, no home, and lived off the generosity of others (2 Corinthians 8:9).

The Apostle Paul also endured incredible hardships and financial difficulties (2 Corinthians 11:23-27). He had a sickness or affliction from which he prayed for relief, but he never received it. God told him that it was better for him to live with the infirmity and learn to trust Him on a daily basis (2 Corinthians 12:7-10).

In Scripture, *God emphasizes* that the best thing for us is to develop Christlike character rather than enjoy financial prosperity. Proverbs 16:16 says,

> How much better it is to get wisdom than gold!
> And to get understanding is to be chosen above silver.

Likewise, Proverbs 15:16 says,

> Better is a little with the fear of the LORD, than great treasure and turmoil with it.

Furthermore, God specifically commands us not to strive to be rich. It's not that wealth is inherently evil, but that we humans are so prone toward greed. First Timothy 6:9-12 illustrates this:

> Those who want to get rich fall into temptation and a snare and many foolish and harmful desires which plunge men into ruin and destruction. For the love of money is a root of all sorts of evil, and some by longing for it have wandered away from the faith, and pierced themselves with many a pang. But flee from these things, you man of God.

It is not just preachers in the prosperity movement who foster a love of money and material gain. Many people in the related positive thinking movement encourage the same warped values. I'm familiar with a prominent multilevel marketing company that encourages its salespeople to dream of cars, houses, and yachts, and to put pictures of furs, Winnebagos, and airplanes on their refrigerators, so that they will long for these items and visualize having them. At the same time, the company brings in a religious emphasis that God wants these salespeople to have their material dreams. The company's whole concept is to cultivate a lust for more! That's something the Scriptures clearly condemn. As Hebrews 13:5 says,

> Let your way of life be free from the love of money, being content with what you have; for He Himself has said, "I will never desert you, nor will I ever forsake you."

Prosperity Theology commonly equates the United States with Old Testament Israel. It tries to apply all the promises God gave the people of Israel to Christians in North America today. That is a major blunder of biblical interpretation. It's as if I promised to mow your yard, then your neighbor said, "Well, I'll claim that promise for my yard, too!" Just because I make a promise to you, in no way means that someone else can claim the same thing for himself.

In a similar way, God made specific promises to Israel that do not apply to us in North America today. I'm not proposing that we throw out the Old Testament. On the contrary, we should treat it for what it is—God's eternal Word. But we must be careful not to wrench the text around, trying to make it mean what it does not mean.

Prosperity Theology reflects an arrogant attitude toward those who are poor—an attitude that God condemns. For surely it is arrogant to say that God promises us wealth when so many of His people are poor.

I recently read of a young woman who taught Prosperity Theology. She had gone to Ethiopia and seen the poverty there. She had seen Christians struggling to be faithful to God. Those people had enormous faith and commitment to God. They claimed many of the simple promises that her teaching said they should in order to become rich. Yet they were incredibly poor. In fact, many were starving to death!

This incident caused the woman to seriously rethink her theology. In fact, after study of the Word and prayer, she eventually stepped out of that ministry. She found that the prosperity view isn't true, and it doesn't work around the world.

Sure, it plays well in the United States, which has abundant natural resources and a stable government and economy. But elsewhere, this view doesn't hold water. It must sound terribly arrogant to the many, many people in other lands who are faithful to God, yet live in deep poverty.

In short, Prosperity Theology paints a picture of the Christian life as one of self-centered indulgence framed in self-righteousness. It implies that our lust for more and more material wealth is not only okay but pleasing to God and ordained by Him. It's a very unfortunate twist on the issue of success. In fact, I think it's worse than the secular view. It's one thing not to know God's perspective on success, or to be confused and leave it out of your thinking, or even to know it and ignore it. But to be familiar with God's Word and then to twist it around, trying to make Him say almost the opposite of what He has said—especially in the service of greed and self-indulgence—that is a heinous offense that mocks the truth of God.

Needless to say, you'll want to avoid this dangerous heresy. It's a facade of spiritual truth—attractive on the outside, but when you turn down the side streets and examine it from all angles, you find only empty ruins.

Fortunately, God has spoken rather clearly on what true success is all about. I invite you to consider His perspective and turn to the next chapter.

PART TWO

True Success

CHAPTER FOUR

How to Succeed Where It Really Counts

E veryone wants to succeed in life. I don't know anyone who doesn't. Yes, we all seem to have slightly different ideas about what success looks like. But in our heart, each of us wants to win in life; we all want to see our dreams come true.

I don't see normal human ambition as either unhealthy or immoral. But it's terribly important that before we give our lives to a pell-mell pursuit of success, we understand clearly what success is and is not. Since God has created us and this world, and since He's spoken about what matters in life, I believe we would be utter fools to ignore or disparage His perspective.

Yet, in its estimation of what success is all about, our culture has done precisely that. It reminds me of a student I had when I was a flight instructor—*Cyrrhus.*

CYRRHUS

As a captain in the Air Force, I was an instructor in the advanced jet training program, flying the T-38. The T-38 was a supersonic fighter trainer. It is still used for training by the Air Force today.

My assignment on one particular mission was to take a solo student out on a precision formation ride. This would involve flying two T-38s three feet apart, just under supersonic speed, through a wide range of maneuvers. Our goal would be to execute a formation takeoff, fly out to the practice area, perform several maneuvers, separate, rejoin, fly back to the base, and land.

Now that's exciting enough, but the student that I was to fly with on my wing in the number-two position would be solo; this would be his first attempt at this type of mission. So for more than an hour, I briefed my student on every last detail of the flight. We went over and over every minute of the mission, until I was certain he was ready. Then we suited up and started to head for the planes.

Just as I was about to leave the flight room, my commanding officer stopped me. "Sherman," he barked, "your student's been reassigned to another instructor. You'll be flying with someone else."

"But, sir!" I protested, "I've briefed the mission with him. We're ready to go."

But it was no use. I would be flying with a different student. Well, I'd just started to get over that when I found out who the other pilot was—a student named Cyrrhus.

Now, to say that Cyrrhus was an inept pilot would be to brag on him! He just didn't have the "right stuff," and I think prior to coming to pilot training, the most sophisticated thing he'd ever ridden was a bicycle. So there was no way I wanted to have him on my wing—not at 500 knots, three feet away! But I didn't have any choice; he was assigned to me, and that was that.

We walked out the door toward the planes, and I was so anguished that I started praying intently: "Lord, I'll do anything if You get me through this!" Perhaps you've prayed that prayer! Anyway, we got out to the aircraft and, believe it or not, things went pretty well at first. Cyrrhus started his engines right on time. He made a sharp, clear, before-taxi radio call to the tower. We taxied out pretty much together, which is a feat in itself. We were cleared for takeoff, and he even lowered his canopy in sync with mine. I was impressed. It looked like a lot of precision. I thought that maybe my prayers were being answered!

We lined up on the runway. He took his three-foot spacing. We ran our engines up. I gave the signal for brake release, and we went right into afterburner. A thousand feet down the runway, though, I glanced in my rearview mirror, and Cyrrhus was nowhere in sight! He missed the signal. As my nose came up, I saw him way back on the runway. I almost scrubbed the mission right then, except he suddenly went into afterburner and came zooming off the runway.

Now, you have to realize that by this point, I was at about eighty percent thrust, while Cyrrhus stayed at 100 percent. And he never let off! He came zooming right at me! At the last second, I veered off, and he shot past me. Then, when I went to rejoin, he pulled back to about sixty percent, and I shot past him. He powered back up to full bore, and we dodged each other like that for the next minute or so. It was awful. We were like a gaggle of geese. Not nearly the precision you'd see with the Thunderbirds!

Somehow we got out to the practice area. We more or less performed our maneuvers. Actually, it was sort of

Cyrrhus avoidance maneuvers. After that, we separated and set up to practice our rejoin.

A rejoin is a tricky procedure—one aircraft quickly ascends to rejoin its companion circling above it. Ours began with Cyrrhus at about a 1000-foot spacing. At that distance his aircraft looked like a small white dot on my canopy. I set up a stable turn, and his goal was to come in and regain the three-foot spacing before we'd head back.

I watched Cyrrhus as he came in. And what started out as just a small dot grew big in about two seconds! I jerked the stick back and executed a hard, 5-G climb as he flew right through my airspace! Had I not done that we both would be pushing up daisies today in west Texas!

I was so mad. I figured, that's it! Enough! We're going to cut our losses and head home. We're going to abort the mission. So I told Cyrrhus to follow, and we headed back to the base.

Air Force pilots have an ego thing about looking sharp as they arrive at a base. And instructors are always judged by their peers on the performance of their students. So I was hoping that Cyrrhus wouldn't do anything stupid that would embarrass me in front of my friends.

As we got to the base, we separated for our landings. I was to take my landing first, and Cyrrhus was to come in about thirty seconds behind me. While I was on my rollout, I cleared with the tower and waited for Cyrrhus to do the same. There was nothing. The tower called him, and still nothing.

Suddenly, I heard this incredibly loud alarm in my headset, and immediately realized what it was: Cyrrhus had executed an absolutely flawless approach with one exception. He forgot to switch the little handle that lowers the landing gear! When you forget to do that, an alarm comes on that almost blasts you out of the cockpit. Cyrrhus' alarm had come on frequency, blaring so loudly that it hurt my ears. I can't imagine what it must have been like for him!

In the T-38 we touch down at a little over 170 miles an hour. The aircraft is usually filled with about 2000 pounds of JP-4, an extremely flammable propellent, and the bottom of the plane is made of magnesium. So, it's really unwise to leave the gear up!

By then the controller was screaming at Cyrrhus, but old Cyrrhus kept coming. They started shooting flares that put off a huge cloud of red smoke, but still he kept coming. Finally, the controller shot a flare right at the cockpit. Cyrrhus was so blinded that he pulled up at the last second and went around. Eventually the tower was able to talk him down, and he landed safely.

Meanwhile, I went to the squad room and waited at my desk for Cyrrhus to come in. And he came in all right—G-suit slung over his shoulder, he looked like Top Gun! The crazy thing was, he had a face full of teeth—absolutely ear-to-ear with a big, cheesey grin. He dropped down in the seat in front of me, smiling away. He was so proud of himself. It's a tribute to the grace of God that I kept my hands off of him! I was furious, but I stayed cool and began my debriefing. I said, "Cyrrhus, the first thing you need to know is that you flunked this mission. You failed the ride!"

Well, he turned livid! He couldn't believe I'd possibly fail him on the ride. After all, he said, he'd done well on his pre-flight. He had a good before-taxi radio call and taxied out with me in formation. He lowered his canopy on cue and took the proper position for takeoff. He even filled out his paperwork when he got back.

Finally I cut him off.

"Cyrrhus," I said, "you did very well at the peripherals, but you failed at the most important task that you had before you. You didn't fly the mission the way it had to be flown." With that he walked out, convinced that I was unfair in my evaluation.

The story of Cyrrhus is amusing (though to me it wasn't at the time). I look back on it now and just have to laugh. Interestingly, it forms a sort of parable about success.

You see, Cyrrhus did well at the peripherals: He did a fine job of getting to the plane, starting his engines, lowering his canopy on cue, having a clear voice check, and even filling out the paperwork. He did well at the *peripherals*, but he failed in the crucial aspects of the ride. As a result, he failed the mission.

I find that when it comes to success, a lot of people *do well at the peripherals*, but they *fail in the essentials.* Many in our culture are doing a great job of making money. They're racking up impressive career achievements. They're taking on more and more responsibility and control over projects and people. They're even surrounding themselves with all the comforts and conveniences anyone could ever imagine. But when it comes to their character, their relationships, their marriages and parenting, or their intimacy with God, they're failing! They're as reckless and disoriented and dangerous as Cyrrhus was in that T-38. And yet, they think they're doing great!

How wrong they are! Money, recognition, power, and a comfortable lifestyle are just the peripherals in life. Nice to have, but not critical. What's essential? Let's find out by looking at a parable that Jesus told in Matthew 25.

THE PARABLE OF THE TALENTS

Near the end of His earthly ministry, Jesus was asked by His disciples to tell them about the future (Matthew 24:3). They were especially curious to know when and how He would set up His Kingdom—in which He would rule over the world, bringing justice, goodness, and right living. In response, Jesus gave an extended discourse, telling several parables (stories that illustrate important truths).

One of them is the parable of the talents. We could just as easily call it "the Parable of the Three Managers," for it is about a wealthy man who entrusted his possessions to three slaves—really managers. Jesus used this parable to caution His listeners about the essentials in life, about what really matters—in other words, about success. Let's begin in Matthew 25:14-15:

> "For it is just like a man about to go on a journey, who called his own slaves, and entrusted his possessions to them.
>
> "And to one he gave five talents, to another, two, and to another, one, each according to his own ability; and he went on his journey."

Three employees were each given a certain amount of money called a talent. A talent was rather valuable. Based on what we know about first-century coinage, a talent might be worth $1,000 or so today, but it probably represented considerably more than that. A day's wages were accounted in denarii, worth about sixteen to eighteen cents each, and a talent was worth 6,000 denarii. So, even if it calculates to only $1,000 to us, it would represent *6,000 days of wages* to Jesus' listeners.

So when the parable says that the man "entrusted his possessions" to his slaves, it means he really handed over the store! To the first he gave five talents—more than that slave could have earned in eighty years of common labor! The second slave received two talents—more than thirty years' earnings. And to the third slave he gave one talent—about sixteen years' earnings.

These three slaves were given enormous responsibility. I don't know how much money you earn in a year, but imagine having that much cash to invest. In fact, imagine having between sixteen and eighty times your annual income to invest! What would you do with the money? Let's find out what the slaves did with it (Matthew 25:16-18):

> "Immediately the one who had received the five talents went and traded with them, and gained five more talents.
>
> "In the same manner the one who had received the two talents gained two more."

Can you just see the picture! That first slave couldn't wait to get started. We can well imagine that he had watched his master doing deals, day after day, piling up his enormous fortune. In fact, it's clear that the slave had helped this man in these dealings, or he would never have been entrusted with so much responsibility in the master's absence. He is called a slave, but he was really a manager owned by the master.

The first manager was apparently a real deal maker. Notice how it says he "immediately" started trading with the money. As soon as he and his companions waved good-bye to their master, he was on the move, lining up contacts, scoping out opportunities, sniffing out bargains. So industrious was he, and so proficient, that by the time the owner returned, he had doubled an already enormous fortune.

In a similar way, the second manager doubled his share. He probably didn't have quite the business savvy of the first manager, since he received only two talents, but he still knew how to make money. The parable doesn't say that he traded with his share. Perhaps instead he put it in safe, conservative municipal bonds and watched it grow. At any rate, he did a fine job of turning thirty years' worth of wages into sixty!

Then there was the third manager. Who knows what went through the master's mind when he handed him his share of the money? Probably the same thoughts I had when I found I'd be flying with Cyrrhus! That owner probably had his doubts about giving this slave the responsibility. But to be fair and to give him a chance, he handed him one talent.

We can guess that this was more money than that third manager had ever seen. For years he'd probably watched the master and the first manager driving in the chariot, turning deals right and left. He'd doubtless heard of the incredible profits cascading in, but he'd never been a part of the action. He'd probably even complained to the second manager about how he was never asked to go along, and if only the master would give him some "real money," why he'd show everybody how to clean up!

Now he had his chance. So what did he do? He put the money—sixteen years' worth of wages—in a sack, slipped out to his little garden, dug down a couple of feet, and buried the whole wad next to the garlics.

Time passed. We don't know how long, but the passage (25:19-21) goes on to say,

"Now after a long time the master of those slaves came and settled accounts with them.

"And the one who had received the five talents came up and brought five more talents, saying, 'Master, you entrusted five talents to me; see, I have gained five more talents.'

"His master said to him, 'Well done, good and faithful slave; you were faithful with a few things, I will put you in charge of many things, enter into the joy of your master.'"

Picture the three managers standing in front of the mansion as the master's caravan arrives. Everyone's in a festive mood. Preparations begin for a big welcome-home dinner. The first manager steps forward to shake the old man's hand enthusiastically, certain that he will be pleased with the doubling of his money. The second greets his master warmly, quietly confident that he will be praised for his performance. Then there's the third manager, who just stands there, grinning, totally oblivious to how the master will respond to his negligence.

The master sets up appointments with each of the three managers. We can imagine something like a breakfast meeting with the first one. The manager brings in the books and starts to go through them, but the master cuts him short: "I can look through those later. Tell me, how'd we do?"

The manager sits back, smiles, and tells him he's doubled the man's money. The master pauses, sets down his fork, and erupts in victorious joy. Doubled! No wonder he shouts, "Well done, good and faithful slave." The two of them laugh with joy — the master for his good fortune to have such a worthy and effective manager, the manager over delight in his master's commendation.

Then the master promises to reward him with more responsibility: "You were faithful with a few things, I will put you in charge of many things."

We don't know what those "many things" are to be, but based on the numbers we've seen so far, we can well imagine they will be an incredibly vast responsibility. Perhaps the manager will take over his master's international operations, maybe he'll become the chief operating officer, but whatever the owner has in mind, he's certain that he can rely on this manager.

So the master adds a final summary: "Enter into the joy of your master." I'm not sure what the man intended by that. Perhaps it meant that the manager was no longer a slave but was free. Perhaps it simply was a way of restating, "Well done!" It obviously means that the master was thoroughly pleased with this man and looked forward to a close, satisfying relationship with him.

The first slave leaves, and the master spends the rest of the morning shaking his head with delight and disbelief. Doubled! Perhaps he begins writing up a new job description outlining the scope of the manager's new responsibilities. At any rate, the second manager arrives for his lunch hour appointment. Knowing that the owner is a busy man, he has prepared a one-page financial summary. But as he hands it to his master, he cuts to the bottom line (Matthew 25:22):

> "The one also who had received the two talents came up and said, 'Master, you entrusted to me two talents; see, I have gained two more talents.'"

The manager scans the sheet quickly to assure himself of its accuracy. Then he drops the page and explodes with delight (verse 23):

"Well done, good and faithful slave; you were
faithful with a few things, I will put you in charge
of many things; enter into the joy of your master."

Notice that the master praises and rewards this
second manager in similar fashion as the first. The
amount of money did not matter nearly so much as the
competence of the manager. He, too, had doubled his
master's money, but he had earned something far
greater—his master's trust!

Well, the two no doubt had an enjoyable lunch.
Perhaps the master recounted his delight with the first
manager's performance, and then included this second
man in his overall evaluation of the outfit's performance:
"You boys have done one incredible job. Before I left I
thought I was rich, now I really know what it means to
be rich! I've not only got a ton of talents, I've got guys like
you to depend on. I'm a truly blessed man!"

The afternoon passes, and toward the end of the day
the master's secretary buzzes him to say that the third
manager has arrived for his appointment. No doubt the
master is curious to see what he will turn in. It's been
such a good day already—five additional talents from
one manager, two more from the other. Who knows,
maybe this third manager will pleasantly surprise him.
Let's look at his report (Matthew 25:24):

"And the one also who had received the one talent
came up and said, 'Master, I knew you to be a
hard man, reaping where you did not sow, and
gathering where you scattered no seed.'"

Not exactly a way to win friends and influence
people! This manager starts off on the defensive. (Maybe

the master writes it off as poor presentation skills.) But things start sliding downhill fast (verse 25):

> "And I was afraid, and went away and hid your talent in the ground; see, you have what is yours."

With that the slave lays on the desk a dirty, soggy sack of coins, reeking with garlic. The master just stares at it, stunned. His neck tightens up. His jaw sets. The veins on his forehead turn turgid and purple. He starts heaving with deep breaths, and finally, leaps to his feet (verses 26-27):

> "But his master answered and said to him, 'You wicked, lazy slave, you knew that I reap where I did not sow, and gather where I scattered no seed.
> 'Then you ought to have put my money in the bank, and on my arrival I would have received my money back with interest.'"

The master seems to spit with unbridled rage! And why not? The slave has been completely negligent. Not only has he not done the simplest thing to make money—putting the money in the bank—he has *cost* the man money, because he's been on the payroll all this time and hasn't earned a dime to pay for himself. That's why the master calls him lazy.

He also calls him wicked. And here's the core of the third slave's problem: He didn't even try to be faithful in the responsibility the master gave him. Apparently this slave had an attitude problem—his failure to perform as expected was in defiance of his master. His failure wasn't just a case of benign neglect; it was willful negligence. He chose to squander his opportunity.

It is his undoing. For the master quickly called in his aides and rendered judgment (verses 28-30):

> "'Therefore take away the talent from him, and give it to the one who has the ten talents.'
>
> "For to everyone who has shall more be given, and he shall have an abundance; but from the one who does not have, even what he does have shall be taken away.
>
> "And cast out the worthless slave into the outer darkness; in that place there shall be weeping and gnashing of teeth."

The worthless slave is not only fired, he's ruined! For the rest of his life, he'll never be able to find a decent job again. He has destroyed his life.

No doubt as the security guards escorted him off the property, the master could hear him crying out, reminding everyone of the good things he'd done, pleading for mercy. Perhaps he pointed out that he had emptied the garbage every night, that he had watered the camels when it was his turn, that he had really been diligent to say, "Yes, sir" and "No, sir" to the master. He had even slipped lumps of sugar to the master's horses every night and supplied garlic to the kitchen!

But like many people today—this rascal had done well only at the peripherals. He'd utterly failed at the essentials! And that's why the guards took him down to the docks and bought him a one-way ticket out of town.

TRUE SUCCESS

The interpretation of the parable of the talents is fairly easy. Given the context, it's obvious that the master is analogous to Christ. Just as the master went away on a journey, so Christ has gone away to His Father, and will return someday to consummate the establishment of His Kingdom. In the meantime, He's entrusted responsibilities to us, just as the managers in the parable had responsibility entrusted to them.

As we look at the master's responses to each of the three managers, we learn to distinguish what is essential in life from what is peripheral. What matters in the parable, and what matters for us today as we await Christ's return, is *faithfulness*. In fact, the success or failure of the managers is determined not by the amount of money they either were given or earned, but by their faithfulness and diligence to carry out their master's wishes.

This brings us to what real success in life is all about: True success means *faithfully pleasing God with the resources and responsibilities He's given us.*

Like the managers in the parable, each of us has been given considerable responsibility by God—not just token assignments, like giving a few dollars to charity or showing up at church two or three Sundays out of four. He has given us enormous responsibilities that are freighted with significance, both for now and eternity.

Think for a moment about your job. We saw in the preceding chapter how much God cares about the job you do. Your work may not seem to matter much to others, perhaps not even much to you, but it matters deeply to God. It's a gift from Him; in fact, it's a trust that He's given you to accomplish His purposes in this world by serving the needs of people. Whether you realize it or not, whether you work like it or not, God has given you a privileged position as His coworker.

How faithful are you in your job? I didn't ask how

"successful," as our culture measures success. You may be making good money, moving up the career ladder, and making quite a name for yourself—but those are just peripherals. How *faithful* to God are you in the essentials: Do you do your work with excellence? Are you competent? Do you get the job done? Are you honest with your boss, your coworkers, and your customers? When you commit to do something, do you fulfill your word? Do you give an honest day's work for an honest day's pay? What's the quality of your relationships on the job? Can you be trusted? Do you resolve conflicts in a prompt, healthy manner? Do you show compassion for the failures, weaknesses, and difficulties of others? Do you pray for people at work?

I could list dozens of other questions that deal with the essentials of work as God defines them. All have to do with faithfully pleasing God in the work arena.

What matters is pleasing God! Do you want to succeed where it counts? Do you want to finish your life and hear the Master pronounce, "Well done," as He surveys your time on this earth? Do you want true success? It can be yours. It comes from faithfully pleasing God with the resources and responsibilities He's entrusted to you.

You can see how radically different this view of success is from what the business and professional world says success is all about. Our culture measures success in quantitative terms. God looks at the quality of our lives —not the quality of our lifestyles, but the quality of our character and the quality of our relationship to Him, to our spouses, to our families, and to those with whom we live and work. Our world focuses on career success almost exclusively; God looks at the entirety of our lives and measures them by His Word. Our culture's form of success is built on comparisons to one another; Jesus Christ looks at the individual, unique character of each person. These are two radically different ways of measuring success.

Of course, the real questions you want to ask are: What does God see when He looks at you? How will He evaluate you when you stand before Him someday? Will you be like the first two managers—confident that your faithful service will reward the trust He's placed in you? Or will you be like the "wicked, lazy" slave—indifferent to God's will, squandering the valuable treasures He's given you?

If you long to hear God's praise, and to enter into His joy, then I encourage you to move on with me to the next chapter. We'll look more closely at how to cultivate faithfulness before God, and find true success.

CHAPTER FIVE

Three Steps to True Success

A man stopped by a computer store where he'd recently purchased a personal computer. "I have a question about a computer I bought here the other day," he said to a salesman who greeted him enthusiastically.

"What kind did you buy?" the salesman asked.

"A Superlogic," explained the customer.

"Model 1200, 1600, or 1800?"

"Uh, I'm not sure. I think it was the 1600."

"Well, that's pretty important, you know," explained the salesman. "They're each configured differently, even though they look the same. The 1200 has a 32-array schnitzelbit that transforms the clock speed from five megs to about fifteen. That means it can handle a million more gigazucks a second than the 1600 or 1800.

"Of course," he continued, "you don't have the same display with the 1200 as the other two. How big is your monitor?"

"Well, maybe about like this," said the man, forming the size with his hands.

"Oh, the big one. You must have the 1800. Unless

you got a special monitor with your machine?"

The man paused. "Well, I, uh, I don't think so."

"Yeah, probably an 1800. That box has a great color board on it. Have you tried color graphics yet? You get around 16,000 tones, with an infinity of gray-scale values. It's really something!"

The salesman noticed that the customer didn't seem enthusiastic about the computer's capabilities. He was looking around and starting to edge toward the door. Not wanting to let any potential sale get away, he finally asked, "Well, how can I help you? Do you need some add-ons? More memory? An accelerator board? How about a graphics pad?"

"Actually," the customer replied, "I just want to know where the power switch is to turn the foolish thing on!"

Have you ever had an experience like that? You ask someone what time it is, and they start explaining how a watch works! You ask a car buff how to change your oil, and he gives you a lecture in advanced hydraulics! You just want to breathe, and someone gives you a theory of air!

Well, so far in this book we've looked at the conceptual, theoretical side of success. We concluded in the last chapter that true success means faithfully pleasing God with the resources and responsibilities He's given us. The question that lingers is: How can we do that? How can we faithfully please God, not only in our work, but in all the arenas of life? What practical steps can we take to achieve true success? Where do we get started?

Obviously, pleasing God is a lifelong process, not just a one-time event. It's impossible to tie it all up in a neat formula. But I can suggest three steps—three principles—that are absolutely essential in the process. Taking these steps doesn't guarantee success; but you must take them if you ever hope to enjoy true success.

CULTIVATE A CLOSE, INTIMATE RELATIONSHIP WITH CHRIST

If you want to please God with your life, the place to start is with knowing God. It's hard if not impossible to please God if you don't know Him. Especially since He's done everything necessary to make it possible for you to know Him, and He longs to enjoy an intimate relationship with you.

A personal relationship with Jesus Christ involves knowing Him as a friend. If Jesus were to come into the room right now in person, would you feel comfortable enough to walk right up to Him, welcome Him by name, worship at His feet, and address Him as Master? Would you be able to exclaim, "I've known You all these years, and now to see You—what a privilege!" Or, would you just hang back, like a stranger, waiting for someone to introduce you? Would you even recognize Jesus if you met Him?

If you sense that you're a stranger to Christ, then I have good news, though there's some bad news to face first. First, you need to recognize that you—like every other human being—have fallen short of God's will for your life. Simply stated, you've offended God. Everyone has! Murder, rape, and grand larceny may not be your style, but envy, anger, deceit, lust, and revenge likely are. Furthermore, not only has each of us committed wrongs, we've failed to do some of the right things we should have done.

I'm sure that's no news to you. The Bible calls these moral failures "sins," and explains, "For all have sinned and fall short of the glory of God" (Romans 3:23). Actually, specific sins are merely the outward symptoms of a deeper, fundamental problem: Every person sins because every person starts out estranged from God, actually in outright rebellion against Him.

Assuming that this is not news to you, you can well imagine that for a crime, there must be a penalty. The penalty of sin is separation from God—living apart from His life, His power, and His love. Like the separation between a corpse and a living person, humanity is separated from a relationship with God as a result of sin. Sin has caused a kind of death in the relationship between God and mankind. Romans 6:23 describes that death, "For the wages of sin is death."

Fortunately, there's good news, too. The good news is that Jesus Christ came to pay the penalty for you, so that you might enter into a personal relationship with God. That's why Romans 6:23 goes on to say, "But the free gift of God is eternal life in Christ Jesus."

Many people complain that God seems to be a distant, cosmic force rather than a close associate. That distance is the penalty for sin. Christ came to remove the penalty for you. First Peter 3:18 puts it this way:

For Christ also died for sins once for all, the just for the unjust, in order that He might bring us to God.

As a result, Christ offers us a relationship with God as a free gift. The Bible calls this relationship "eternal life." This relationship is given as a gift to those who trust Christ to take away the penalty of sin.

Perhaps as a child or sometime during your life you heard John 3:16:

"For God so loved the world, that He gave His only begotten Son, that whoever believes in Him should not perish, but have eternal life."

This verse, among other passages, urges you to decide today to put your faith—your confidence and trust—in Christ for eternal life. It's a bit like putting your faith in a pilot to fly a plane for you—just as you trust the pilot to do something you can't do for yourself, so you trust Christ to do something for you that you can't do for yourself. It's an important decision that you must make; no one can make it for you. You must come to the point where you are able to tell God something like: "Jesus Christ, I place my trust in You to do something for me that I can't do for myself; that is, to take away the penalty of my sin and to give me eternal life. I believe in You."

The words, of course, are not the important thing here; the trust that you place in Christ and the attitude of returning to Him are. It's the beginning of a new relationship with God. In fact, it's the most important decision you'll ever make, the most important choice anyone could ever make. To decline God's offer is to leave yourself estranged from Him. You'll never find true success apart from Him.

Making a decision to enter into a relationship with Christ is merely the start of the relationship. Once you've made that decision, then you need to cultivate that relationship—the way you would any friendship. Remember, you can't please God if you don't know Him. The more intimately you know Him, the more you'll want to please Him.

Cultivating intimacy with God is a lifelong process. Let me suggest three habits to develop to help you in that process. First, you'll want to spend some period of time alone with Him every day. Give some of this time to simply appreciating Him for who He is and what He's done in your life. Also lay yourself open before Him, telling Him your concerns, hopes, fears, hurts, failures, needs, and aspirations. There is no substitute for this one-on-one time when it's you and God, just the two of you. If you want to know God, spend time with Him.

A second important habit is to admit to God when you've done something to offend Him, and apologize for it. You wouldn't expect to be intimate with your spouse if you never apologized to him or her when you've done something wrong. The same applies to your relationship with God. If you catch yourself lying, or gossiping, or even neglecting God, stop and deal with that before Him. Such things don't end your relationship with God, but they do shut down your intimacy with Him until they're dealt with. So deal with them, remembering that God is extremely gracious and understanding (Psalm 103:8-11):

> The LORD is compassionate and gracious,
> Slow to anger and abounding in lovingkindness.
> He has not dealt with us according to our sins,
> Nor rewarded us according to our iniquities.
> For as high as the heavens are above the earth,
> So great is His lovingkindness toward those who
>   fear Him.
> As far as the east is from the west,
> So far has He removed our transgressions from us.
> Just as a father has compassion on his children,
> So the LORD has compassion on those who fear
>   Him.
> For He Himself knows our frame;
> He is mindful that we are but dust.

A third habit that builds intimacy with God is to practice what is true and right—in other words, to obey God. This is not simply a matter of knowing the right things or giving mental assent to the correct beliefs. It's a matter of life-change. Jesus is not particularly impressed by people who know a lot of Scripture and a lot about Scripture, and yet Scripture makes little difference in their lives. On the other hand, He's wildly enthusiastic about you if the little you know makes a big difference in how you live (John 15:10-11):

> "If you keep My commandments, you will abide in My love; just as I have kept My Father's commandments, and abide in His love.
> "These things I have spoken to you, that My joy may be in you, and that your joy may be made full."

The first step to true success is to cultivate an intimate relationship with Christ. That relationship begins when you trust Him to take away your sin. It grows into an intimate, valued companionship as you spend time with Him daily, as you deal quickly and regularly with offenses you commit against Him, and as you practice His truth and let it change your life. To please God you must know Him, but you must also know what it is that pleases Him. That brings us to the second step in the process.

LEARN GOD'S ASSIGNMENTS FOR YOUR LIFE

Success before God means faithfully pleasing Him with the resources and responsibilities He's given you. To be faithful in this way requires that you know what those resources and responsibilities are. It's not just what you think they are, it's what God says they are. Pleasing Him involves allowing Him to set the agenda for your life.

I'm amazed, though, at how limited some people think that agenda is. In chapter 3 I described the Two-Story view of life and work that divides life into sacred and secular categories. This view has caused many people to think that God's interests boil down to daily prayer and Bible reading, church attendance, and ethical behavior, with an occasional extra effort as a volunteer for a charity or involvement in evangelism. If you do those, you'll usually be considered as a strong Christian.

What a limited, narrow, faulty view of life! The fact is, *every* aspect of life is to be lived out with an eye to God's will and pleasure. Colossians 3:17 tells us,

> Whatever you do in word or deed, do all in the name of the Lord Jesus, giving thanks through Him to God the Father.

That's pretty all-inclusive. The concept is that Jesus Christ is Lord over all of life—not just a narrow band of personalized activity that we call religion. Whatever we do in life, we're to do it "in the name of the Lord Jesus"—under His authority, with a purpose of pleasing Him.

Furthermore, when we examine the teaching of the New Testament, we find that it addresses five major categories of life:

1. *Personal life*—including one's relationship to God, his emotions, and all of the private, individual, inner aspects of his life.
2. *Family*—including one's spouse (if married), children, parents and other extended family, and

any dependents.

3. *Work*—one's employment or occupation, how he earns a living (for career homemakers, homemaking is their work).

4. *Church* life—one's relationships both near and far to all those in the family of God.

5. *Community* life—one's responsibilities as a citizen toward the government and his relationships in the broader society and the world, especially with those outside the faith.

Five major areas of life. Bill and I discuss these areas in considerable detail in *How to Balance Competing Time Demands* (NavPress, 1989). I encourage you to obtain and study that book. It goes hand-in-glove with what we're considering in this book; and it develops this five-pronged, New Testament view of life fully.

Focus on this point: *A successful life is one that pursues a measure of faithfulness in each of those five areas.* It's not only church or spiritual life that matters, as the Two-Story view holds, nor is it just work that matters, as so many in our society believe. God has specific assignments for us in each of the five areas. To ignore any one of these areas is to ignore our responsibilities before God. What do I mean by "assignments" and "responsibilities"? Here are some examples.

In Your Personal Life

God has given you a relationship with Him as a tremendous privilege and resource. Are you growing in that relationship by feeding yourself on "the pure milk of the word," as it says in 1 Peter 2:2? Are you eliminating filthy speech and off-color jokes, as Ephesians 5:4 encourages?

Your physical body is also a valuable resource from

God. Are you maintaining yours? Are you treating it like a temple, in which God Himself has come to reside (1 Corinthians 6:19-20)? Are you giving it enough rest and sleep (Psalm 127:2)?

In Your Family

If you are married, your spouse and children are enormously valuable treasures entrusted to you. Are you providing for their material needs, as 1 Timothy 5:8 commands? Are you weaving God into their lives, as Deuteronomy 6:6-9 encourages? Do you date your spouse regularly as a way of cultivating intimacy (see Ephesians 5:33)? Do you control your children, building into them a healthy sense of discipline and respect for authority (Ephesians 6:4)?

Even if you're single, you still have family responsibilities, according to the New Testament. For instance, are your elderly parents' material needs provided for (that's the context of 1 Timothy 5:8)? Likewise, even if you don't have children of your own, God wants you to be concerned with the needs of orphans (James 1:27). You should always work on building a godly character and a healthy way of relating to people—necessary even if God doesn't call you to marry and have children.

In Your Work

We've seen that work is a valuable gift from God. Are you doing all you can to hold a steady job that provides for your needs (2 Thessalonians 3:6-15)? Do you submit to the authority of your boss and company rules and standards (1 Peter 2:18)? Do you put excellence into your job, as Ephesians 6:7 encourages? Is your "workstyle" so unique and exemplary that it earns the respect of co-workers and wins a hearing for the gospel (Titus 2:9-10)?

In Your Church

Others who know and follow Christ are another important resource given us by God. Do you regularly worship
with other believers, as Hebrews 10:25 commands us?
Do you encourage others in their faith and walk with
God (Hebrews 10:24)? Do you use your gifts and talents
to help the Body of Christ grow (Ephesians 4:16)? Do you
financially support those who teach you God's Word and
help you grow in the faith (Galatians 6:6)?

In Your Community

God also has very specific assignments for you as you
relate to the broader community. Do you obey the law—
for instance, driving within the speed limit (Romans
13:1-2)? Do you pay your taxes honestly (Romans
13:6-7)? Is your lifestyle winsome and attractive in repre-
senting Jesus Christ to unbelievers (1 Peter 2:12)? Are
you eager to help the poor, as Paul was (Galatians 2:10)?

There are scores of other assignments God has for us
in these various areas. It's critical that you read and
study your Bible so that you'll know what these assignments are. Then start fulfilling them.

You'll not change overnight; but you can improve a
little each day. This process of learning how to be faithful
in the five areas will gradually change your character
and your lifestyle. You'll stand out. Your enthusiasm for
the Lord will be contagious. Your purpose in life will be
clear.

At your job, for instance, you may work just as hard
as others, but you'll do it for different reasons. You'll
desire to bring glory to God in your work, not to feed
your own ego. Your integrity will change as you commit
yourself to fairness and telling the truth. You'll follow the
rules. You'll develop skill in relationships. Excellence

will become the hallmark of your performance.

Your self-image will also improve as you come to appreciate God's love for you in creating you, sustaining you, and bringing you to Himself. You'll come to love yourself in a proper, healthy way. You'll sleep at night, knowing that while others may have out-performed you, you play by different rules—God's rules.

Maintaining faithfulness to God is one of the toughest challenges you'll ever face. But you learn to live the Christian life by doing it. Each day, you must take specific steps to apply Scripture to your life. It takes discipline, desire, and determination, but God has promised to help if you ask.

COMMIT YOURSELF TO LIVING WITH A GODLY VIEW OF SUCCESS

Remember, the first step toward true success involves knowing God, and the second involves knowing God's assignments for you in each category of life. The third step in the process involves acting and choosing from a godly view of success. This book presents a whole new way of living, thinking, and working. If you want to become a success where it really counts—before God—then you have to commit yourself to living with a different outlook than your surrounding culture. Later, I'll talk about some of the new freedoms, values, and ways of making decisions that this biblical view of success provides. But first, let me summarize what it means to commit yourself to a godly view of success.

A Commitment to Christ's Lordship
Our culture has come to a day when everyone is his own boss. We may technically work for others, but when it

comes to running our lives, we expect independence and freedom. In fact, it's become an unspoken assumption that each of us has the right to determine what is right or wrong for himself, without interference from others. Individuals follow no absolute authorities anymore. Instead, we're encouraged to do our own thing in our own way. Nowhere is this commitment to radical individualism more in force than in the careerism that reigns in today's workplace.

But if you intend to pursue godly success, it's obvious that self-rule must give way to Christ's rule in your life. The two are diametrically opposed. Success in our culture means faithfully pleasing *oneself* with the resources and responsibilities one's been given. By contrast, true success before God means faithfully pleasing Him with our lives.

This means that Christ calls the shots. It doesn't mean avoiding responsibility and acting like we're brain-dead or getting into weird, mystical schemes for discerning God's will. We still have choices to make—tough choices, at times—that God won't make for us. But when I say that Christ calls the shots, I mean that it's His desires, His interests, and His agenda that ultimately matter to us—those are what we need to fulfill.

Let me illustrate. A friend of mine owns an especially lucrative business. Several years ago he and his wife went to see a strategic planner to help them chart their course for the rest of their lives. For the better part of a morning, the consultant listened to them talk about themselves, their goals and aspirations, and what they wanted out of life.

Finally, he took out a piece of blank paper and drew a small box at the top of it. Out to the side he wrote two words: *Jesus* and *money.* Then he looked at the couple and said, "From what you've told me this morning, there are two major forces that have powered your life up to now. But as I see it, you're at a point where one *or* the other has to have priority. Now, you tell me which one of these words to put in the box, and I'll tell you how to map out a strategy. If you want Jesus in the box, fine; I'll show you how you can organize your life around Him. If you want money, I can show you how to do that. Which word do you want in the box?"

According to my friend, that room was quiet for about three or four minutes. The couple didn't say a word to each other; they didn't need to. They realized that they had come to a fork in the road where they were going to have to decide which agenda mattered—the financial interests of their business, or Christ's. Furthermore, the person who had articulated this turning point was not a preacher or minister with vested interest in the outcome, but a highly-paid strategic consultant who had no interest in religion and no concern with their choice one way or the other.

I'm glad to report that the couple chose to put *Jesus* in the box. By their own testimony, it's made a most profound difference in the course of their lives ever since. They chose a commitment to Christ's lordship. Is that what you are prepared to do? Or is Christ to be merely an add-on to your life, the caboose on a train driven by career success?

A Commitment to Life-Change

I want to underscore the fact that "faithfully pleasing God" is an activity, not just a nice set of beliefs. It must be a way of life.

This is so incredibly important in our day! Twenty years ago, people were asking the question: Does God

exist? Today that question has changed to: What difference does He make? The answer for too many people is:
Not much. Even for many people who have an enormous
amount of Bible knowledge, God makes little difference
in how they actually live their lives.

Therefore, I think it's fair to ask: If Christ doesn't
make any difference in my ethics and values at my job; if
He doesn't affect my speech and attitudes toward coworkers; if He doesn't change the way I resolve conflicts,
or how I serve other people; if He doesn't keep me from
pilfering company supplies, or from using the company
phone for personal long-distance calls and company
postage to ship personal parcels, or from copying pro-
tectively licensed software; in short, if He makes absolutely no difference in the way I live and work, then pray
tell, what difference *does* He make?! What's the point of
playing a religious game that is all talk and no action?

I take the matter of *obedience as an action* quite
seriously. I challenge you to do the same. Whenever
you're exposed to Scripture, ask yourself: How can I
apply this to my life? What practical thing can I do to
embed this truth in my attitude, character, and behavior? Where does it need to make a difference? That's a
commitment to *life-change*.

A Commitment to Ethical Purity

I'll say much more about ethical purity in the following
chapters. Here, I just want to point out that our culture
operates more and more on the ethics of expediency.
People used to do what it took to get the job done. Today
they'll do *whatever* it takes to get it done—ethics be
damned!

But with God there are no ethical shortcuts. I know
there seem to be gray areas where it's hard to slice right

and wrong cleanly. But the person pursuing godly success makes every effort to figure out how much purity he can keep—not how much impurity he can get away with.

If doing what's right ultimately means walking away from a deal, or a job, or even a career—so what? Yes, it's hard. Yes, it hurts. Yes, it shouldn't have to be that way. But the fact is, while integrity sometimes costs, lack of integrity costs even more. It costs us deeply in terms of true success. Proverbs 3:32 spells out the alternatives pretty clearly: "For the crooked man is an abomination to the Lord; but He is intimate with the upright."

If you want intimacy with God, you must commit yourself to ethical purity, no matter what it costs. After all, we follow noble men and women who have followed Christ, even at the cost of their lives! So what is the loss of a few dollars, a few notches up the career ladder, or even a loss of income by comparison? Psalm 37:16-18 promises,

> Better is the little of the righteous
> Than the abundance of many wicked.
> For the arms of the wicked will be broken;
> But the LORD sustains the righteous.
> The LORD knows the days of the blameless;
> And their inheritance will be forever.

A Commitment to Godly Decision-Making

We each have to make choices in life—choices about who we'll marry, what jobs we'll take, where we'll live, and so on. Our culture's view of success encourages self-centered decision making—take the highest paying job, marry the most well-connected person, live in the most prestigious neighborhood. Society says to *always* make contingency commitments—agree to something, until something better comes along.

Obviously if you desire true success, the world's approach to decision making won't do. Instead, you'll make choices in light of God's agenda for your life. For instance, you'll evaluate how your decisions affect all five categories of life, as we discussed earlier. You'll also consider any Scripture or biblical principles that might have a bearing on the situation. Consequently, you'll consult with others who know and love God—wise Christ-followers who can offer godly counsel.

Ultimately, you'll pray carefully about major decisions, asking Christ to help you honor Him as you make your choices. Once you commit yourself, you'll keep your word, even if you find that it costs you to do so.

A Commitment to Trust God for Outcomes

By now you know that your life succeeds or fails on the basis of your faithful service to God in the areas He's designated for you. What happens when that faithful service seems to result in defeat rather than victory? Or in hardship rather than prosperity? That's the point at which you have to trust God entirely for the results.

At the beginning of chapter 3, I told the story of Allen, a landscape architect in a down economy, with few opportunities left for his firm. If I had talked to Allen about his alternatives, I would have discussed the practical things he could do to hang on. I could never have guaranteed that his firm would make it. But I would have challenged him: (1) to see that God cared about what happened to him and the people he employed; (2) that his work mattered to God; (3) that he had a responsibility as an employer to do all he reasonably could to find work for his firm; (4) that there were obvious limits on what he could and should do, because so much was beyond his control; and (5) that he needed to trust God for the outcome of his business. God might choose to keep it going by providing opportunities; He might choose to shut it down.

I identify enough with Allen to know how awful it would feel to finally have to say, "Enough. I quit. I'm getting out." Some people would say that Allen should pay whatever price is necessary to see that his business succeeds; in fact, that's the only way it will succeed. But biblically, that's hard to justify. Biblically, God wants us to hold onto career success with a light touch. Whether we succeed or fail—or fall somewhere in between—so much is out of our control that we must do our best and leave the results to God.

I'm not talking about evading our responsibilities. Rather, I'm talking about forgoing the presumption that our success in life ultimately is dependent on ourselves—that we are the masters of our own fate. That's sheer fantasy. James warns against believing this lie:

> Come now, you who say, "Today or tomorrow, we shall go to such and such a city, and spend a year there and engage in business and make a profit."
>
> Yet you do not know what your life will be like tomorrow. You are just a vapor that appears for a little while and then vanishes away.
>
> Instead, you ought to say, "If the Lord wills, we shall live and also do this or that."
>
> But as it is, you boast in your arrogance; all such boasting is evil. (James 4:13-16)

In summary, three steps lead to true success: cultivating an intimate relationship with God, learning God's assignments for your life, and committing yourself to living out a godly view of success. Remember that these describe a lifelong process, not an event.

That process yields enormous benefits, which people chasing the world's idea of success will never know. In part three, we'll examine what some of those benefits are.

A New Way of Life

New Freedoms
New Values
New Ways of Making Decisions

New Freedoms

My father was a bomber pilot during World War II. He commanded a B-17 and flew many sorties over Nazi-occupied territory.

During one of his raids over Berlin, his plane caught flak and lost the use of three engines. Limping back on the one remaining engine, he realized that his aircraft could never make it to England. He finally ditched the plane in the Netherlands, which was held by the Nazis.

He was captured and sent to a prison camp—Stalag 13, as it turned out. But, as you can imagine, it was no *Hogan's Heroes* comedy! It was a grim terror filled with uncertainty.

Imagine the feeling for my dad and the other prisoners when they looked out one day and saw General George Patton's tanks sweeping across the fields, coming to seize the camp and liberate the prisoners! What a sense of joy and freedom must have gripped them! Their ordeal was over. They'd be going home. They were free at last!

In our culture many people are imprisoned by a

flawed view of success. Perhaps you are. Perhaps you've sold out to the empty promises of ambition, only to find yourself enslaved to a harsh taskmaster.

If so, you need the liberation that comes from adopting God's perspective on success. God wants you to enjoy true success, and the true freedoms that come with it—wonderful freedoms that most people will never know, but will envy. In the next four chapters, we'll focus on new freedoms that a godly view of success offers.

CHAPTER SIX

The Freedom to Enjoy Life

I don't know what your daily commute to and from work is like. Perhaps you drive in rush-hour traffic, take a train or a bus, or catch a shuttle flight to a distant city. But where I live—about twenty miles outside of Washington, D.C.—if I have a 7:00 a.m. appointment downtown, I have to leave my front door by 5:30 at the latest. That means I have almost an hour and a half of stop-and-go driving.

Whatever your commute is like, have you ever looked at the expressions people wear as they head to work? Have you ever tried to read what's going through their minds? Do you suppose they're thinking, "Boy, I just can't wait to get to the office! People there are so interesting and exciting to work with. They're like all these hundreds and thousands of people jammed in around me in traffic—so wonderful and special, each one just like a Christmas gift waiting to be opened and reveal its surprises!"? Do people think like that on their way to work?

How about on the way home? Are they thinking,

"What a fantastic day this was! It was wonderful to be able to make my contribution to the company. I really appreciate that opportunity. It's a joy to serve people through my job, people like all these hundreds and thousands of folks jammed in around me—special people who make the world a great place to live!" Do you suppose people think like that on their way home?

Of course not! In the main, people commuting to and from work look grim—mighty grim! There's something on their minds. They have their game faces on. There's a tension in their furrowed brows and nervous ticks. Their haste and impatience with delays reveals an agenda that's driving them.

What is that agenda? What is it that drives people back into rush hour morning after morning? I wouldn't presume to speak for everyone on the road, but I've spoken with enough workers and observed enough about myself and others to know that vast numbers of us are driven by anxiety about career success.

Pete was driven. Pete was a custom home builder. One day he told me that he was discouraged and feeling somewhat insignificant. We talked about it awhile, then I learned that earlier in the day a competitor had come to meet him at one of his job sites. In the course of their conversation, the man mentioned how many homes he was building and how quickly they were going up.

As Pete listened, he realized he was not building nearly as many houses, nor was he able to build them as quickly as his competitor. As a result, he came away from the discussion feeling demoralized and insignificant.

Why? I believe it was because Pete, like so many people in our culture, was measuring his worth as a person by his success in his career—success measured by the *number* of homes under construction. Anyone who measures his worth that way will inevitably be discouraged and feel insignificant. In fact, they'll feel tremendous anxiety to succeed, because every time a new set of numbers comes out, every time a sale is pending, every time the stock market rises or falls, their identity will be on the line.

How about you? Is your life wrapped around the axle of career success? Is your identity on the line each morning as you head into work? If so, you need to discover that God's view of success offers *freedom from anxiety about career success to an enjoyment of work and leisure.*

How do you see your job? One woman saw hers as a proving ground. She had two kids and was a career homemaker—until her husband walked out on her. She felt so humiliated and furious that she put her kids in day care, picked up a job as a secretary, put herself through law school, and eventually joined a thriving law firm. Day after day she poured herself into her job, determined to prove that she was just as competent, confident, and self-sufficient as any male lawyer in the practice.

Through a set of circumstances, she discovered one day how addicted she was to her career. She realized that her reason for being there was not merely a love of law or a concern for justice, but a personal agenda for proving her worth. In her anger and humiliation, she had sold herself out to an unhealthy ambition. Eventually that ambition turned her workplace into a grim stalag where success was not something that would be nice to have, but something she *had* to have.

What a complete reversal on God's intentions for work. Ecclesiastes 5:18 tells us that God intended work as a gift:

Here is what I have seen to be good and fitting: to eat, to drink and enjoy oneself in all one's labor in which he toils under the sun during the few years of his life which God has given him; for this is his reward.

Enjoyment of work is actually a reward. How sad it is that our culture turns work into a burden through its slavish preoccupation with career success.

God wants to free us from that. He's given us talents and abilities that He wants us to use in the workplace. He never intended that arena to be a testing ground where our egos are constantly having to prove themselves. What a pleasure it is to go to work when you realize: "I don't have to prove anything to anybody! God has already established my worth. I'm free to use my abilities and skills to accomplish His agenda, not mine."

Can you see how this freedom allows you to focus on faithfulness to God, rather than just results? Not that you should take a careless attitude, or give up trying to win; no one wants to do that. No one should. But winning or losing is no longer the most important thing. Instead, character and a Christlike lifestyle become priorities, because they form such a major part of true success.

A friend of mine illustrates this well. He stuck a considerable sum of money in a mutual fund run by a "friend," who turned out to be both negligent and deceptive. As a result, this investor lost nearly sixty cents on the dollar for every dollar he invested!

Naturally, he used every means at his disposal to recoup his investment, or at least cut his losses. But in the end, he took a real beating. I asked him one day about what he learned from the experience. He looked me in the eye and said, "One of the things I've seen as a result of losing this money is that it really doesn't matter. It just doesn't matter."

I know this man was telling the truth. He had come to the point where he realized that whether he scored big in an investment or lost it all, the outcome is not what matters. Not ultimately. Sure he hated to lose that money—anyone would. Sure he thought about what he could have done differently, and how he might have invested more wisely—that's understandable. But when the deal went sour, his world didn't fall apart. He was enjoying the freedom that a godly view of success offers—freedom from anxiety about career success and an enjoyment of work and leisure.

That same freedom can be yours. It comes when your ultimate goal on the job is not winning—not achieving impressive numbers, not overwhelming your peers with your accomplishments, not proving your superiority—but rather, faithfully pleasing God.

CHAPTER SEVEN

The Freedom to Balance Life

Larry was a motivational speaker associated with a management consulting firm. He had come to the position out of a background in sales and marketing. Before joining the firm, he was already enjoying plenty of success at a Fortune 500 company. But friends and acquaintances kept telling him, "Larry, you're so good up in front of people, you should be on the seminar circuit."

For a while Larry had laughed these suggestions off. Sure, they were nice compliments, but he had a stable job that provided an above-average lifestyle for his family. Why risk that?

Then Larry was asked to handle a couple of workshops at a regional industry convention, which he did. At the conclusion of his first session, people crowded to the front, mobbing him with questions. It was obvious they'd enjoyed his talk and found it helpful. By the time Larry arrived to lead his second workshop, word had spread, and he was greeted by a standing-room-only crowd. Again, the response was overwhelming.

Larry was flattered by it all. It made him feel a new sense of expertise and confidence. But really, it was not unexpected. He'd always had a way with people, which is perhaps why he was doing so well in his career.

A few weeks later Larry received a call from an official at the trade group that had sponsored the convention.

"Larry," he said, "the evaluations on your presentations at last month's show were outstanding, probably the best we've ever seen. We'd like you to do that material again for the national convention next fall. How about it?"

Without really thinking, Larry agreed to be there. It was more than he'd expected. And when he delivered his workshops again, the response was more than he expected. People stood in line waiting to talk with him afterwards. One man asked him if he'd published any books yet. He was astounded when a trade publication reporting on the convention put a prominent photo of him on its cover.

Soon he was getting calls from other groups to come speak. Then the management consulting firm contacted him. Maybe it was the weather, maybe it was the time of day, maybe it was the impressive salary range they quoted, but Larry agreed to meet and talk about a possible move to that firm. In the end, he left his job in sales and hit the road as a motivational speaker.

And he was good! Audiences across the country flocked to hear him. Clients told the firm he was the best they'd ever had. Soon he was limiting his talks to crowds of no less than 300 people—then 500. The firm kept raising his salary. Then they began hiring people dedicated just to serving him.

About that time a major publisher approached him

with a contract for a book series. All he had to do, they said, was to keep doing what he was doing. They'd transcribe his talks and have a ghost writer massage them into manuscripts. With almost no effort on his part, he'd soon be swimming in royalties!

Next came the video producers. They told him just to do his thing, and they'd tape it and package it into a series that he could sell at a huge profit. The cameras rolled, and he was a smashing success, a real natural.

The crowds grew larger. Invitations piled up. More publishers called. More producers stopped by. A newspaper syndicate asked whether he'd consider doing a weekly column. A major audiocassette distributor asked to handle his tapes. Associates in the industry called to ask for his endorsements.

Larry kept on speaking. What started out as one two-day seminar per week quickly grew to two. Then he re-packaged the material into one-day events—Mondays through Fridays he was on the road. He also spoke at evening banquets, which because he did them on his own, were all profit. Weekends were spent answering mail, reading reports and publications, and handling details. In the end, he was working seventy hours a week, usually more.

Was Larry successful? You bet! Certainly when measured by our culture's standards. But somehow in the midst of this dizzying parade of opportunities, his life began to unravel. The first signs of trouble occurred on a road trip when a woman invited him to dinner following the day's seminar.

Larry felt odd going out to dinner with a complete stranger in a distant city away from his wife. But he rationalized it as "consulting" and determined to keep the conversation strictly professional. And he did. The two spent the entire evening and well into the night discussing his work and how he felt about it. Then they parted.

What he failed to admit to himself afterward, however, was how special he felt disclosing himself to this woman. She seemed to take a keen interest in what he did, and she asked perceptive questions that yielded insight into himself and his abilities. The fact was, he'd been able to tell this woman things about himself and his career that he'd never been able to verbalize to his wife. And she'd understood him so well. Thus began a form of emotional adultery, which estranged Larry from his wife and nearly brought his marriage to ruin.

He didn't end up as a total tragedy, as others like him have, but he did go through an incredible amount of pain. Today he rarely speaks at seminars; and he never travels alone. Some people would still say that Larry achieved smashing success. The question is, however, on what basis? Certainly, he performed unusually well in his career; but that is not all there is to true success.

Larry illustrates what happens when a person gets hooked on success. When Larry was in sales, he had felt reasonably successful, well paid, and rather happy. What upset this arrangement, of course, was the speaking he began to do at conventions.

"But he did that so well!" one might protest. Indeed, he did it extraordinarily well, maybe too well for his own good. It was a tremendous boost to Larry's ego every time he was asked to speak.

At first it was just flattery. But when he gave his first workshops, he underestimated the response—and how good that response would feel. It felt even better after the national convention. And by then he was just about hooked on it. What began driving his life was not a concern for the needs of his listeners but a craving to have his ego stroked. He quite literally became addicted to the response of crowds, with the attention of certain women feeding this unhealthy habit.

Larry is an extreme, to be sure. Yet there are many of us like Larry who get work out of perspective because it is so satisfying to our ego.

When I was a boy my family had a little poodle, just a tiny thing. When I came home from school, that dog would greet me and beg for dog biscuits—the sort of disgusting "treats" that only a dog could love. I'd take a biscuit and hold it in my hand about waist high, and the dog would jump up and grab it out of my hand. Then I'd hold another one up about level with my eyes, and he'd jump up and get it. It was amazing how high he could get. Then I'd hold one way up above my head—and he'd bite my foot!

We went through that exercise every afternoon, and that dog just loved it. He was addicted to those dog biscuits. I find that a lot of us are addicted to the "ego biscuits" we get at work. They may be something as simple as the approval of our boss or recognition at a company banquet, or as big as a fat year-end bonus or a promotion, but they feed our ego and pride. Though they start out as just pleasant surprises, those ego biscuits can become addictive, enslaving us to the relentless demands, opportunities, problems, and challenges of our careers. We become like the man who admitted, "I know my work is killing me. But I love what I do!"

If that's your situation, then you need to discover that God's way of success offers *freedom from frantic busyness and overwork to a balanced lifestyle*. Consider what such a balance would look like in three areas.

First, it involves balance in the area of *commitments* and *expectations*. Bob is a salesman. He's busy all the time. In fact, he's too busy. Everyone wants a piece of Bob's time, and he gives it to just about anyone who asks. As a result, he is very, very busy.

Every time I talk to Bob's wife, she complains that he's too busy. She never sees him. His boss wants him to work on Saturdays. His kid's soccer coach wants him to help coach soccer. His pastor wants him to be a deacon and to teach Sunday school. The salesmanship club wants him to chair a committee. Even his eighty-three-year-old mother wants him to come sit with her on Sunday afternoons!

Bob's problem is that he's trying to please everybody. Not only can he not do that, he shouldn't even try! True success means faithfully pleasing God with a balanced use of our time. God realizes we have limited time, so He encourages us to set limits on our commitments.

Limits? God wants limits? You'd never know it, judging by the expectations that seem to cascade down on us through sermons, Sunday school classes, books, videos, and so on. In fact, Bill and I sometimes wonder whether we're not adding to the pressure people feel through books like this one!

Yet the fact remains, God really demands far less from us than we sometimes imagine. Sure, many people could stand to exert themselves far more in terms of their spiritual development, but others of us feel overloaded with responsibilities and expectations. We need to know that God is not asking us to do more; He's asking us to do *less* and to trust Him more. This is Jesus' point in Matthew 11:28-30:

> "Come to Me, all who are weary and heavy laden, and I will give you rest. Take My yoke upon you,

and learn from Me, for I am gentle and humble in heart; and you shall find rest for your souls. For My yoke is easy, and My load is light."

Of course, if you're overwhelmed with demands, a passage like this one can sound like wishful thinking. Reading it, you may feel, "That would be nice to have, but it'll never happen to me!" In that case, you may already be far down the same road Larry took, driven by an insatiable hunger for ego biscuits, resulting in frantic busyness and overwork. God calls such a frenzied lifestyle "vain." Notice Psalm 127:2:

> It is vain for you to rise up early,
> To retire late,
> To eat the bread of painful labors;
> For He gives to His beloved even in his sleep.

Are you able to put the work of the day aside and get a decent night's sleep? Or, are you so consumed with commitments that you rob your body of rest and resort to caffeine or other stimulants and strategies to keep all the balls in the air? Bill and I discuss this problem of achieving a strategic balance among your commitments in *How to Balance Competing Time Demands*.

Faithfulness to God means that you can't have unlimited goals and expectations in any one area of life—particularly work—without injuring other areas. Yes, you need to set goals and make commitments—but not unlimited goals and commitments. Remember, God desires a measure of faithfulness in your personal life, family, work, church, and community. This requires balance. You can't have unlimited goals in your career and still build a solid marriage. You can't have unlimited commitments to the programs of your church and keep your job. You can't spend all your time with your spouse and kids and ignore your personal needs. Life doesn't work that way.

God wants to free us from the need to make unlimited commitments, from the need to please everybody, from the need to satisfy every demand. When our focus is on faithfully pleasing Him, we can say no to many, many good things in order to enjoy the best thing—a healthy, balanced life lived to His glory, not ours. We may not win any popularity contests, but our goal is not the approval of others, but the approval of God.

Another aspect to a balanced lifestyle is balance in the area of *excellence*. Colossians 3:23 instructs us to "work heartily"—to really put our heart and soul into our work. But the question arises: In what way? There's a real distinction to be made between the effort we expend on the job and the results we obtain.

Most people put their heart into achieving excellent results. It's the product that counts. But is that altogether wise? For as workers, we have limited control over the outcome of our labors. So much is out of our hands—the attitudes and performance of coworkers, the decisions and demands of our boss, the interest in and demand for our product or service, the state of the economy, the weather. Sometimes despite our best efforts, the results turn out pretty mediocre, or they don't turn out at all.

I believe God wants us to concentrate on excellence of effort rather than on excellence of results. Not that we don't strive for outstanding results, but our main concern lies with doing the best job we can, "as for the Lord" (Colossians 3:23).

We need to be able to stand before the Lord and say, "I may not have done my job perfectly, and the outcome may not have been exactly what I wanted. But I did as well as I could with the resources and responsibilities You gave me."

Recall the second manager in the parable of the talents. His results were not as impressive as the first manager's—he had less to work with, too—but he was faithful! He achieved excellence of effort. That's what we need to accomplish. That sort of faithful service earns a "well done," even if it doesn't produce the outstanding results that others seem to achieve.

God also wants to set us free from frantic busyness and overwork through a balanced use of *emotional energy*. I've observed that most careerists invest about ninety-five percent of their emotional energy in their work. Work is all that seems to matter to them. Family, God, friendships, the society around them—they give about five percent of their concern to all these areas combined!

Elise was like that. She regularly worked a fifty-hour week as a computer software designer—those hours increased considerably when she was in the middle of a project. But whether she worked forty hours or eighty, she was consumed by her job. At home, she went through the motions of preparing meals and doing chores. Often when her husband would ask her questions, she'd be working out a design problem in her mind. On weekends he'd suggest an evening out, but she'd beg off, preferring instead to stay home and read career-related publications. At church she found her attention wandering back to details of work projects, rather than concentrating on the sermon.

In short, like Elise, many people allow the very excellent job they do in their careers to absorb nearly all their emotional energy. Unfortunately, the price for this extremely single-minded focus can be steep: neglected spouses and friends who slowly drift away, either in spirit or in fact; neglected children who grow angry and frustrated by their parent's relentless preoccupation with work; or perhaps a neglected walk with Christ, with a loss of intimacy and the resulting vulnerability to spiritual attack.

God never intended work to become the sole focus of our lives. When it does—when it captures all of our emotional energy—then work becomes an idol, a god that rules us. In contrast, when we adopt a godly view of success, our focus becomes faithfully pleasing God in every arena of life. As a result, we can put work in its proper perspective with the rest of life, and divide our emotional energies accordingly.

CHAPTER EIGHT

The Freedom to Care About People

Have you ever known anyone who is always comparing himself to everyone else? Laura has. Laura was a sales rep for a large jewelry manufacturer. She had a coworker, Mark, who was always checking to see how he was doing in comparison to the others on the sales team, especially Laura.

Mark would review the sales reports religiously to see where he stood. Every time, he was one or two slots in back of Laura. During one period, the sales manager held a contest with very attractive incentives. At the end of the contest, he posted the results for all to see. Laura had placed high, though she was not the leader. Still, she was satisfied with her performance, and the small award that would be coming her way.

Coming out of the conference room where the bulletin was posted, she ran into Mark, just coming in from his last sales call. Mark didn't need to see the scoresheet to know how he'd done—he'd been methodically tracking that from the start. But he did ask Laura how she had done, and when she told him, he threw up his arms, screamed, and walked away! Mark had also placed high in the contest—but his score was five points less than Laura's.

Mark was gripped by a kind of bondage in comparing himself to Laura. He was like so many people in our culture who measure themselves and their worth against those around them.

Many people compare abilities, and always seem to find someone who can do the job just a bit better, or faster, or more skillfully, or more lucratively, or less expensively than they can. They compare performance, and always find someone whose performance is better—more precise, more well-received by others, more perfect—than theirs. They compare their position and status to others, and inevitably find someone with more personnel under them, more authority, more prestige, or more friends in high places than they have. They compare their wealth and possessions with those of others, and always find someone with a more expensive house, a more prestigious vacation spot, a better education for the kids, or a more lucrative investment than they have.

Such is our culture's view of success. It inevitably leads to comparisons. In contrast, God's view of success provides *freedom from comparing ourselves to others to a concern for others*. This is an incredible freedom to have in a culture that measures success on the basis of external, insignificant factors.

Tom illustrates this well. He went to a company party at his boss's lake home. The home itself cost nearly three million dollars. For three million dollars, you can get a *nice* lake home. Of course, that was just for the house. The ski boat and the sailboat in the private marina were extra, as were all the furnishings in the home. They were not ordinary furnishings, either, but a professionally designed decor with magnificent works of art and sculpture. It was an incredible weekend hideaway!

You can well imagine how most of the employees walked around gawking at all this opulence, expressing envy at each new turn: "Boy, I'd like to have a hot tub like this!" or "This bathroom's about the size of my whole living room!" or "Gee, life is really tough; I'm glad I don't have to suffer like this!" You know how it goes. Everyone found himself comparing what he didn't have to what the owner of the business did have.

But Tom was different. Tom had genuinely started to experience freedom from the need to compare himself to others. Undistracted by the costly surroundings, he enjoyed focusing on the people at the party, spending time getting to know them and their needs. After all, the busy routine of the workday rarely afforded him a chance to concentrate on his coworkers as much as he'd like. But in this relaxed atmosphere he had a great opportunity to demonstrate compassion.

That's a great freedom. When our lives are given to faithfully pleasing God, there's no longer any need to compare ourselves to others and what they have versus what we have. Instead, with a clear mind we can focus on people and their needs, as opposed to their possessions. That's the freedom of compassion.

This world desperately needs compassionate people. Our coworkers around us bring incredible needs with them each day. Often those needs are disguised under confidence and attention to their work. But in so many cases, heartbreak and emptiness lie just under the surface—family situations are waiting to explode, past mistakes and regrets that haunt, stresses and strains too embarrassing to admit on the job.

Humans facing such conditions need a Savior. You

and I can't be that Savior, but we know One who is. Often, the first step toward people finding Christ is the Christlike attitude and compassion of a coworker. We can demonstrate that Christlikeness when we're free from the need to measure ourselves against others, and instead offer a compassionate concern for them.

CHAPTER NINE

The Freedom to Accept Yourself

Are you a perfectionist? I find that most careerists—people who wrap their lives around their careers—tend toward perfectionism. I know that Bill and I do; perhaps you do as well. Perhaps the particular work that you do matters so much to you that you won't let it go or give it your approval until it's well-nigh perfect.

Charlene is a perfectionist. She's a graphic designer at an ad agency, working under the direction of the art director, Phil. If you ask Phil about Charlene, he'll tell you that he always gives her the more important jobs because he knows she'll do them right. He admires the way she won't give up on a project until it's perfect—even staying well into the night to meet an important deadline. One morning, for instance, he came in to find Charlene still hunched over her drawing table, just as he'd left her the night before. She was completing a layout that he described as "brilliant." Apparently others agreed, for the project later was nominated for an award.

Charlene's devotion to excellence sets her apart from others in her field. And this drive for perfection doesn't stop with her work. It extends to nearly every other area of her life—her clothes, friends, habits, car, apartment, finances—everything. But since no one is perfect, nor can anyone do everything right all the time, Charlene finds herself quite irritable at times, and harshly critical of herself and others. No matter how good something is, she'll point out the flaws.

Charlene's perfectionism is a problem, but it's really just a symptom of a much deeper problem. Like so many of us, she has never accepted herself for who she is, nor has she found a solid basis for her worth and value as a person. Instead, her estimate of her own and others' worth depends on achievement and performance, which are always less than perfect.

If you can identify with Charlene and you struggle with accepting yourself as you are, you may know how deep-seated this problem is. It pervades your entire outlook on life. Uncovering the roots of this condition and overcoming it go far beyond the scope of this book. (One excellent resource is Larry Crabb's *Inside Out*, NavPress, 1988.) But one ray of hope is offered by the godly view of success we've been considering. In contrast to our culture's perspective, which is performance-based, true success offers *freedom from trying to be perfect to accepting ourselves the way we are.*

Recall our definition of true success: faithfully pleasing God with the resources and responsibilities He's given us. Notice the ways that this concept leads *away* from an unhealthy self-concept. First, the condition of godly success is faithfulness, not perfection.

This can be a very disturbing way of looking at things if you're achievement-oriented. Somehow it doesn't seem right that you could turn in an incredibly high level of performance, and yet God would fail to be impressed by that! If you're a real perfectionist, you probably feel like protesting, "What's wrong with God, anyway? Can't He recognize good work when He sees it?" And if you're really pathological, you might get angry and dismiss God's appraisal altogether: "Look, I do the best job I can, and if that's not good enough for God, well then . . . !"

All of this betrays, however, the true object of your devotion. You're faithful, all right—faithful to some incredibly high standard or image that in your mind represents worthy, acceptable achievement. In a real sense, that high standard is your god; that's what you are dedicated to pleasing.

What a vicious god to serve! It calls for perfect performance, 100 percent of the time, which requires an enormous outlay of energy—and leads to inevitable failure. Furthermore, such a standard is a very shaky basis on which to build your self-worth. So many factors outside of your control can keep you from attaining that standard. And here's the worst of it: Serving images of perfection and performance as a basis for your life is so unnecessary, because God has already provided an infinitely better way.

In God's system, personal worth can not be won or lost through outstanding performance and achievement. It is a gift each one of us inherently possesses because we are people created by God Himself. He has already pronounced that we are "very good"—intrinsically good, of inherent worth (Genesis 1:31). Even in our sin and rebellion against Him, we have not lost that intrinsic value, as God Himself demonstrated by offering up His own Son, Jesus, on our behalf (Ephesians 2:3-10). He considered us to be of such worth that He did everything an infinite God could do to restore us to Himself.

The second way true success leads away from an unhealthy self-concept is that our worth is already *established* by God. How is it *expressed* by us? How do we demonstrate our God-given value as people? Again, by faithfully pleasing Him with the resources and responsibilities He's given us.

One enormous area of resources and responsibilities has to do with our work. In fact, the workplace may be the most visible arena in which we express (not establish) our worth. For it is there that we display our talents, abilities, and skills—gifts that God has given us to accomplish His tasks. When we diligently use those resources to meet the needs of people and to please God, then we are being faithful to God's intentions for work. As Colossians 3:23-24 encourages,

> Whatever you do, do your work heartily, as for the Lord rather than for men; knowing that from the Lord you will receive the reward of the inheritance. It is the Lord Christ whom you serve.

What impact could this have on a person's self-concept? Let's return to Charlene. Charlene's needs are complex and deep-seated, so I don't want to oversimplify. But if she were to adopt the concept that God has already established her worth as a person, that could go a long way toward freeing her from the need to prove herself through her accomplishments at work. She would no longer need to try to make herself acceptable through outstanding achievement.

Instead, she would be free to simply do her best— not to try and prove herself, but as an act of devotion to God. Naturally, her best work would be extraordinarily good work; she apparently has substantial talent. In fact, she might at times appear to work just as hard as before. But she'd be doing it for different reasons. Instead of serving an image of perfection, she would be serving God. At times, faithfulness to Him in her work, given her abilities, might require late hours and other sacrifices. She would not want to turn in a mediocre performance. But she would not be driven by the need to establish her worth, rather by a concern to serve Christ and meet the needs of people.

Is that the sort of freedom you want, the freedom to accept yourself as God has made you? My prayer is that you'll find that freedom, so that your work becomes a blessing you enjoy, not a curse you endure. Remember, God already established your inherent worth when He made you and when Christ died for you. Now He wants you to serve Him faithfully with the many resources and responsibilities He's given you.

We've covered four freedoms that a godly view of success offers:

1. *The freedom of enjoyment*—freedom from anxiety about career success to an enjoyment of work and leisure.
2. *The freedom of balance*—freedom from frantic busyness and overwork to a balanced lifestyle.
3. *The freedom of compassion*—freedom from comparing ourselves to others to a concern for others.
4. *The freedom of self-acceptance*—freedom from trying to be perfect to accepting ourselves the way we are.

In addition to new freedoms, a godly view of success also has a profound impact on our values. We'll consider some of these implications in the next section.

New Values

It's been nearly fifteen years since my wife and I got married. One of the things I've noticed during that time is how profoundly my values have changed.

I remember, for instance, when Jan and I were courting, I loved to ride motorcycles—the faster the better! A while later, after we were first married and I was an instructor pilot, I loved to fly at supersonic speed with another aircraft "bolted" to my wing, three feet away. There was a real thrill to that because of the speed and danger involved.

Today, however, I'm a very different person. I still love adventure, but with a wife and three kids, I'm much less willing to put myself at risk. My values have changed. Whereas thrills and chills used to matter to me, responsibility and security now matter far more.

In a very similar way, my values have changed gradually, but surely, the longer I've known the Lord. I find this to be so for nearly everyone who follows Christ. He slowly teaches us what is important, what really counts to Him. And as He does, our values change.

Perhaps one way to understand this is to think of big fish and little fish. It's important to know the difference. The big fish are the ones you want to catch and keep. The little ones you just throw back.

In the area of values, there are big fish and little fish. When it comes to success, it's interesting to note the contrast between God's values and our culture's. God's list of what matters—His big fish—is almost identical to our culture's list of little fish; and what He considers little fish are almost always big fish in our culture.

Let me show you what I mean as we consider four sets of new values that a godly view of success brings.

CHAPTER TEN

A Value on Integrity

Perhaps you've seen the Academy Award-winning film, *The Killing Fields*. It's a gripping and grim account of the "silent holocaust" that occurred in Cambodia as the Khmer Rouge took power in the mid-70s. As many as three million of Cambodia's seven million people may have been slaughtered by the Communist regime.

In the film, *New York Times* journalist Sydney Schanberg covers the upheaval taking place. Cambodian society is collapsing under the pressures of the Khmer uprising and a confusing American foreign policy. As the city of Phnom Penh falls, the United States evacuates its citizens; but Schanberg stays behind, intent on covering the story, with possibilities of a journalistic award in the back of his mind.

His decision to remain, however, imperils his Cambodian assistant and friend, Dith Pran. Pran's family manages to reach America; but Pran stays behind out of loyalty to Schanberg and his own profession as a journalist.

Once the Khmer take control, however, they seize the two and other journalists. Only through Pran's intervention are the Westerners' lives spared. Eventually they are evacuated, but Pran is turned over to the new regime.

Back in the States, Schanberg's stories indeed result in his winning a prestigious award. At a posh banquet in New York, he makes his acceptance speech. He faults U.S. government policy in Southeast Asia, but clearly his own conscience is bothering him. He explains why the award should be shared by his Cambodian counterpart, Pran (who even at that moment is undergoing sheer torture at the hands of the Communists).

After his speech, Schanberg runs into a photographer who was with him in Cambodia. Acting like the voice of his conscience, the photojournalist accuses him of having betrayed Pran by insisting that they stay rather than evacuate. Schanberg, he charges, was more intent on winning professional recognition than on saving the life of his friend.

Schanberg erupts with defensiveness, but he knows the charge is true. Later he admits to his sister, "He stayed because I wanted him to stay. And I stayed . . . ." He cannot complete the awful confession that he stayed to win an award—at the expense of Dith Pran.

Miraculously, Pran manages to escape the insanity of the Khmer and flee to Thailand, where he and Schanberg are reunited. Today, both work for the *New York Times*.

Many aspects of *The Killing Fields* are compelling. One of the most interesting problems raised is the tension Schanberg felt between commitment to his professional achievement and advancement and commitment to a trustworthy friend. The issue is one of integrity.

I wish more people in our culture were haunted by

questions of integrity. But unfortunately, most ignore such worrys in a mad drive for status and glory. Many athletes, for instance, take steroids—a clear breach of the law and a disservice to their bodies—in order to boost their competitive edge. Salespeople will often encroach on another's territory to make their quota. A businessman slyly applies for and is granted a patent on a device he did not design, then sets up a company to make it and market it—and cuts the actual inventor out completely. A journalist fabricates stories about the inner city in order to win a Pulitzer Prize.

I could go on about the incredible "war stories" I've heard from the marketplace. People want to win so badly that they'll lie, cheat, steal, and even, murder, if necessary, to get what they want. It's a twisted value system from a biblical point of view; but on the street, the game is played by the ethics of expediency. As a jingle composed by recent graduates of the Wharton School of Business (and sung to the tune of Michael Jackson's "Beat It") puts it:

I cheated, I cheated,
And I probably sound conceited,
You're probably angry,
I'm overjoyed,
I work on Wall Street,
You're unemployed.

In God's economy, however, professional recognition is a little fish. It's fine, it's okay, it has a momentary thrill. But the longer you walk with Christ daily, the more you will have *a nonchalance about professional recognition, but a deep concern about integrity*. Integrity is a big fish to God; in fact, it's one of the biggest.

Psalm 15 is an instructive passage along these lines. It's only five verses long, but it speaks volumes about the vital necessity to commit ourselves to integrity. It opens with a question (verse 1):

O LORD, who may abide in Thy tent?
Who may dwell on Thy holy hill?

When you investigate what these images mean, you discover that the psalmist is asking: "Lord, who gets to enjoy a privileged, intimate relationship with You?"

How would you answer that question? Who do you think should get to sit next to the God of creation, sharing His counsel and enjoying His delightfulness? What sort of person?

It's interesting to note who has privileged status in our culture: politicians; sports champions; pop musicians; news anchors; successful maverick entrepreneurs; game show hosts and hostesses; Hollywood stars; and even talk show hosts.

God evaluates people much differently. The psalmist goes on to describe who enjoys intimacy with Him (verses 2-5):

He who walks with integrity, and works
   righteousness,
And speaks truth in his heart.
He does not slander with his tongue,
Nor does evil to his neighbor,
Nor takes up a reproach against his friend;
In whose eyes a reprobate is despised,
But who honors those who fear the LORD;
He swears to his own hurt, and does not change;
He does not put out his money at interest,

Nor does he take a bribe against the innocent.
He who does these things will never be shaken.

There are many fascinating details we could examine here; but one thing stands out: It is the pure of heart who see God. We may be top salesperson of the month, or bill more hours than other lawyers in the firm, or be the first person in our class to make a million dollars—certainly these bring a measure of recognition—but it is our integrity about which God is deeply concerned. *Integrity* is a big fish to Him. How important is it to you?

Recently a salesman attended one of our seminars. He was on the verge of retirement and was involved in a potential sale that would have netted him a hundred-thousand-dollar commission. Not a bad way to go out! The only problem was, in order to make the deal work, he would have to be somewhat deceptive when he presented the product to the customer. Would you tell "white lies" to earn six figures? Is a six-figure fish a big one to you? It seemed pretty big to him.

But as he listened to the seminar presentation, he was challenged to maintain his integrity and let the chips fall where they may. In the end, that's what he decided to do. He told the customer the complete truth, and it cost him the sale.

Was it worth it? He felt it was. Later, he said that he realized that by telling the truth, he could retire with a clean conscience, instead of living the rest of his life with guilt. He knew he'd sleep better at night, and be able to wake up and look at himself in the mirror, with confidence that he'd done the right thing. Most importantly, he'd enjoy his retirement knowing that God was smiling on the decision he'd made.

This salesman proved to be a Psalm 15 man. Sure he

lost some money, and he let a sizable fish get away, but it was a small fry in comparison to his integrity, to a clear conscience, and to the approval of God.

When you look back over the years of your career, and when God looks over it with you, you'll want to be able to smile, knowing that you maintained your integrity. You'll want to feel satisfied that you were a faithful employee, that you told the truth, that you kept clean numbers, and that if you ever did compromise yourself, you were very quick to rectify the situation, to make restitution where necessary, and to right any wrongs you were part of. You'll be able to do that as you cultivate a high value on integrity.

CHAPTER ELEVEN

A Value on Character

O ne of the interesting developments in the business world over the past twenty years has been the increasing importance of titles. In many industries, you can no longer find a salesman or even a salesperson; instead, you can only deal with a "sales consultant" or a "client representative." Some companies are big on vice presidents; it seems like anyone and everyone above entry level is a "veep" of one thing or another.

People must feel slighted if they don't have a title to match their perceived contribution to the organization. That's certainly how Robert felt. Robert had worked his way up to a position of authority in his company. He was called a senior analyst, and he was over several dozen people. But that didn't matter much when his company was sold to a rival, and Robert was out on the street.

For months he tried to find a comparable position. Finally, he was offered a job in another city at a considerably reduced income. The chief sticking point in the negotiations was not the salary, but the title. In his view, this potential employer was asking him to do almost exactly the same thing as his old company, only they called it simply "analyst," as opposed to "senior analyst." Robert asked them to upgrade the title, but they refused.

Back and forth they negotiated, until in desperation, Robert's wife insisted that he forget about the title and just take the job. He did, but whenever he saw his name listed simply as "analyst," he quietly seethed, bitter at what felt like a demotion.

It's easy to see how picayune Robert's objection was if we look at the situation objectively. Yet many of us, in our own fields—each with their unique pecking orders—feel a very similar anxiety about where we stand on the ladder. Surgeons may worry about which operating rooms they get and when. Managers may wonder why some names are listed on company stationery but not theirs. Salespeople may fret about which parking space they've been assigned. Brokers may vie to see which of them gets a corner office in a new building. Executives may complain about not having their names and photos included in the annual report. It seems that every occupation has its rating system, and everybody has a vested interest to see that he gets the prestige and position he deserves. That's one of the bigger fish in the world's view of success.

God, however, seems to take little interest in who's who in the workplace. Instead, He evaluates individuals on the basis of their character. As a result, those who become intimate with God develop *a nonchalance about ladders and titles, but a deep concern with character growth*. It's not the position you hold that matters, but the person you are. That's a big fish in God's perspective.

Most of us are concerned about our reputation, who we are publicly, when everyone's watching. That's important. But what is even more important is our character—who we are privately when no one's watching, and deep down where no one can see. No one, that is, except God. That's why character is so important; it's the person God sees when He looks at us. It's normally a different person than our coworkers or even our families see, because "God sees not as man sees, for man looks at the outward appearance, but the LORD looks at the heart" (1 Samuel 16:7).

What does God see when He looks at your heart? It's certain that He won't see perfection; but it's crucial that He see *growth* toward Christlikeness. Your deep concern should be with character growth.

Character growth involves a changed lifestyle. It means letting go of harmful, sinful habits and adopting healthy, Christlike ones instead. It means a change in the way we relate to others, the concern we have for them, the words we say to them, the way we resolve conflicts with them. It involves our behavior and the choices we make. It means an adjustment in our attitudes and the opinions we allow to dominate us. In short, character change involves becoming different people, Christlike people, in very tangible, specific ways.

This is important to realize because growth has become an almost useless buzzword among Christians today. A lot of funny stuff passes off as spiritual "growth." I've identified a number of fallacies in this regard. Let me mention three.

One is the attendance fallacy. Believe it or not, some folks think that a relationship with God is simply a matter of regularly attending church and church-related programs. It's as if God gets excited that they bother to show up every time the doors are open.

Obviously, church plays a vital role in the Christian life. But imagine an employer giving an employee his annual review and saying, "You know, Bill, you didn't do the job I gave you. You spent your year guarding the snack room, shooting the breeze. In fact, you didn't complete any of your projects. What's worse, you caused our company to lose some of its biggest customers. But, by golly, you were here every day! I could set my watch by you: at half past eight, you'd walk through those doors, day after day. And because of that, I'm going to give you a great big raise!"

No employer would do that! And I can't see God handing out any attendance awards when we come up for final review before Him. His evaluation will focus on our character. Christlike character grows as we make deliberate changes in our attitudes and behavior.

A second misunderstanding about Christian growth is what I call the activity fallacy: If you're busy for God, you must be growing. Consequently, people who hold this view knock themselves out with all kinds of church and volunteer work. Whether all this activity makes them better people, however, is another story. Unfortunately, you can become extremely involved in good, worthy causes without ever changing your character.

A third fallacy (my personal favorite) is the education fallacy: The more you know the better you become. It's as if your head were a bank vault, and every time you hear a sermon or some Bible teaching, you deposit a load of valuables inside. Each time, you add to your treasures and really "grow" as a Christian.

Or do you? Does knowing what constitutes a godly family automatically produce a godly family? Does knowing that you should do your best at work automatically translate into better effort? Does knowing that God despises dishonesty in any form automatically make a difference in how you fill out expense reports, tax forms, and loan applications, or how much ownership you take for an assignment you've botched?

It isn't knowing the right things that produces character, it's *doing* them. Growth occurs when the truth of God's Word makes a practical, positive difference in how I live my life. For instance, when I stop doing things that irritate my wife, I become a better husband and my character grows. When I begin to handle the frustrations that my children present in a gentle, loving, understanding way, I become a better father and my character grows. When I stop pilfering supplies and using the company phone for personal long distance calls, I become a better employee and my character grows.

I certainly want to maintain a good reputation among my professional peers and the public at large. I certainly enjoy the little ego boost that comes from a title and a position. But the big fish that I must not let get away is the growth of my character. It's critical—no matter where I fit on the organizational chart—that every day I take small but deliberate steps toward becoming like Christ. Those are the steps that lead to true success.

CHAPTER TWELVE

A Value on Relationships

In 1968 I entered the Air Force Academy in Colorado Springs. If you think back to that tumultuous year in America's history, you can imagine how odd it felt to be attending a college where the best students vied for a chance to fight in a war that the rest of my generation was protesting!

My perspective has changed since then, as it has for many who marched in the streets. One aspect of the student rebellion of the late '60s that stands out in my memory was the denunciation of materialism. It was popular in those days for kids to reject the upper-middle-class affluence of their parents and follow the counter-culture movement. Money and the multi-national corporations that made and managed it were perceived as the enemy.

It's funny to look back on the slogans and rhetoric of that era. Today, it all sounds so empty and terribly naive. Yet there was a kernel of truth in the anti-materialism message—the idea that people matter more than things. Many college kids were protesting the way in which their parents had emphasized houses, cars, and financial security over relationships, especially relationships with their kids.

Perhaps that's why it's especially tragic to see many from this same generation outdoing their parents in acquiring every gadget and convenience, often at the expense of intimacy with others. Financial status is every bit as important in the '80s as it was in the '50s. In fact, it may be more so.

So many people in our culture see money and the things money can buy as a way of showing off. Having a certain imported car, wearing a certain watch, vacationing at a certain resort—things like these are valued less for themselves than for the statement they supposedly make about the owner. In a word, they spell "success" with a designer label.

Recall our discussion of ego biscuits in chapter 7. We live in a culture where men and women are addicted to little trifles that massage their vanity. No longer are purchases meeting simple, normal needs. Instead, items are bought for status' sake.

God says the pursuit of status is wrong. It's just wrong. In 1 Timothy 6:9-10, the Apostle Paul puts the matter plainly:

> Those who want to get rich fall into temptation and a snare and many foolish and harmful desires which plunge men into ruin and destruction.
> For the love of money is a root of all sorts of evil, and some by longing for it have wandered away from the faith, and pierced themselves with many a pang.

As the author of Hebrews 13:5 states,

Let your way of life be free from the love of
money, being content with what you have; for He
Himself has said, "I will never desert you, nor will
I ever forsake you."

Quite plainly, financial status is a little fish to God.
Obviously money is a part of life, and God expects us to
earn it and use it wisely. But God is not impressed if you
have a lot of money; neither will He snub you if you don't
have very much. In contrast, something that matters
deeply to God is the quality of your relationships. To
Him, people matter infinitely more than things. So if
you adopt a godly perspective on success, in time you
can expect to develop *a nonchalance about financial status,
but a deep concern for relationships*.

Simply stated, the Christian who is weak in relationships is a weak Christian. In many ways, the quality
of one's relationships tell everything about one's walk
with Christ. For instance, consider what Paul told the
Galatian believers. When it came to pointing out the
finer points of doctrine and conformity to Christian
standards, these people were Johnny-on-the-spot. But
their relationships reeked. So Paul warned them, saying,
"If you bite and devour one another, take care lest you be
consumed by one another" (5:15).

In contrast, the believers at Thessalonica, though
not without problems, received high marks from Paul for
the quality of their relationships (1 Thessalonians
4:9-12):

Now as to the love of the brethren, you have no
need for anyone to write to you, for you your-
selves are taught by God to love one another; for
indeed you do practice it toward all the brethren

who are in all Macedonia. But we urge you, brethren, to excel still more, and to make it your ambition to lead a quiet life and attend to your own business and work with your hands, just as we commanded you; so that you may behave properly toward outsiders and not be in any need.

Relationships are big fish to God. Here are five that the Scriptures specifically address. Many others could be mentioned.

YOUR RELATIONSHIP TO THE LORD

We've already looked at how crucial intimacy with Christ is, but I mention it again because it is the foundation on which all other relationships depend.

A couple of years ago, I took my sons camping in the mountains of New Mexico. One bright, sunny morning, I and one of my sons sat on a log by a chattering stream, whittling sticks. The night had been cold, so it felt wonderful to bask in the warmth of the sun.

He and I just sat and talked for about two hours. We talked mostly about things he cared about—like a couple of movies he had seen. We had a chance to just enjoy each other's company. It was wonderful. It had to be one of the highlights of that year, maybe of any year we've had together.

As I've thought back many times to that experience, I've realized that just as I as a father delight in spending special time with my son, so my heavenly Father delights to spend time with me as His son. In practical terms, He enjoys the fellowship we have as I read His Scriptures and hear what He has to say to me. He also likes to hear me pray and talk to Him.

My relationship with God needs to be just as intimate, just as warm, just as wonderful as the relationship I enjoyed with my son by the mountain stream. God longs to enjoy a deep, satisfying relationship with me.

God longs to have the same with you. Are you making time for God? Are you building an intimacy with Him? When you stand before Him someday, will it be without a break in the flow of conversation? Or, are you given to collecting ego biscuits? When you finally see God face to face, will it be like two strangers meeting? If so, you are passing up the biggest fish of all for a few measly minnows. Is it worth it?

YOUR COWORKERS

If I wanted to find out what sort of person you really are, one of the best ways would be to work alongside you for a few weeks. Through the many experiences of the workday, I'd quickly discover what sort of metal you're made of.

Of course, you'd find out a lot about me, too. That's the nature of the workplace: It tests people, and brings out their best and their worst—sometimes, especially their worst. Genesis 1:26 says that God created "every creeping thing that creeps on the earth." Some of us work alongside those creeps, and some of us are creeps ourselves! Seriously, though, your relationships with coworkers are one of the most valuable assets you have, and an important responsibility.

Let me suggest three ways you can pursue faithfulness to God as you interact with others on the job. First, whatever image you project at work, whatever reputation you're trying to achieve, you should make sure that it projects Christlikeness. Titus 2:9-10 (NIV) is addressed to slaves, the largest occupational group in the Roman Empire; but it offers principles for all of us today in terms of our reputations:

> Teach slaves to be subject to their masters in everything, to try to please them, not to talk back to them, and not to steal from them, but to show that they can be fully trusted, so that in every way they will make the teaching about God our Savior attractive.

Did you catch that? "So that in every way they will make the teaching about God our Savior attractive." Paul is describing a person whose lifestyle and "workstyle" on the job are so unique and Christlike that they make the truth about God attractive—winsome, desirable, irresistible.

Is that you? As you do your work in front of the dozens of watching eyes that scrutinize you (they know, after all, that you claim to know God), as you relate to the boss, to customers, and to your associates, are you making Christ attractive or repulsive? There's no question that for many people, you are the only commercial for genuine Christianity they will ever see. Is your life persuasive and compelling?

A related principle is that you should always promote good for others, not evil. Galatians 6:10 reads, "So then, while we have opportunity, let us do good to all men, and especially to those who are of the household of the faith." Some have misinterpreted this passage to say that Christians should receive special, preferential treatment from fellow Christians, but that's not really Paul's emphasis. His point is that we as Christ's people should be marked by goodness—a genuine concern for the rights, welfare, and needs of others.

Nowhere is this benevolent spirit needed more than in the workplace. For many, it's a jungle out there! People lie, cheat, and play the game by very dirty tactics. It's a world that sometimes appears to be motivated by nothing but greed and ambition. And it eats people alive!

You as a Christ-follower could make a difference. While others may be concerned only with grabbing money, your concern can be with people and their needs. While others may trample on the rights and feelings of others, you can stay sensitive and compassionate. While others blow their stacks in anger and look out for number one, you can seek resolution and reconciliation based on what's true and fair.

That brings us to a third area of relationships on the job: the inevitability of conflict. Romans 12:17-18 instructs us how to deal with conflicts:

> Never pay back evil for evil to anyone. Respect
> what is right in the sight of all men. If possible, so
> far as it depends on you, be at peace with all men.

There's real truth to the idea that no one can make you angry. No one can *make* you angry; however, you can *choose* to be angry in response to others. But that's your decision, not theirs. Romans 12 is telling us to choose peace, not anger, and to keep the yard mowed on our side of the fence; we have no control over what happens on our neighbor's side.

YOUR BOSS

Recently, Bill and I were in Canada, and an employer asked us why it is that whenever he hires Christians, he seems to invite trouble in the door. I had to tell him that this is not unusual. Wherever I go, I get asked that same question. It's a tragedy and an absolute disgrace! The shocking fact is that in North America today, people who identify themselves as Christians have a terrible reputation for their poor work ethic and appalling business ethics.

I'm not thinking only of the minority of people who use the label "Christian" as a credential on their calling cards and then do substandard work. They are a complete disgrace to the cause of Christ. But the problem is more widespread than that.

In December 1983, the Princeton Religious Research Center published a landmark survey conducted for *The Wall Street Journal* by the Gallup organization. The researchers measured a wide range of moral and ethical behaviors, such as calling in sick when not sick, cheating on income tax, and pilfering company supplies for personal use. In reporting their findings, they stated that they could discern no significant difference between the churched and the unchurched in their ethics and values on the job.

I regularly receive confirmation of this distressing situation. Just the other day, for instance, a lawyer, who attended a conference I spoke at, reported that "already this week, in response to my explanation of the legal standard required to obtain certain relief, one 'Christian' client proposed to me, that, 'Although it would not be ethical, couldn't we just make up whatever the court wanted to hear?' Another 'Christian' client proposed not to sign or perform the documents that recorded earlier oral promises."

The lawyer concluded, "In my experience, non-Christian clients do no better on these issues." (And no worse, I might point out from Gallup's report.) "Of course, I face these temptations myself. We all have plenty of opportunities to demonstrate our ethics."

Don't we ever! That's why your relationship with your boss is such a serious thing. In a very real way, the reputation of Christ Himself is on the line when you show up for work. Earlier, we looked at Titus 2:9-10. Recall that we were exhorted to do our work in such a way that we would "make the teaching about God our Savior attractive."

Are you making the gospel attractive by your work-style? A great place to begin is with your boss. The reason is because bosses represent authority, and authority so often seems unreasonable. Consider 1 Peter 1:18-21:

> Knowing that you were not redeemed with perish-
> able things like silver or gold from your futile way
> of life inherited from your forefathers, but with
> precious blood, as of a lamb unblemished and
> spotless, the blood of Christ.
>
> For He was foreknown before the foundation
> of the world, but has appeared in these last times
> for the sake of you who through Him are believers
> in God, who raised Him from the dead and gave
> Him glory, so that your faith and hope are in God.

What might this look like in practical terms? It starts with showing up to work on time, prepared to work. It means giving an honest day's work for an honest day's pay. It means staying until quitting time, not slouching out the back door fifteen minutes early.

It also means responding to your boss with respect and courtesy; even if you can't always respect the person, God asks you to respect the position. It means working diligently and efficiently—not only when the boss is looking, but just as much when he's not around. It means respecting company property and equipment. It means abstaining from pilfering company supples. It means resolving conflicts as best as you can, making apologies and amends where you've been in the wrong. It means carrying out the tasks you're assigned in a trustworthy, reliable manner. It means fulfilling your word when you make commitments. It also means praying for your boss and his needs and issues.

In short, it means acting as Christ would act were He in the job you have. Could that affect how you go to work tomorrow morning? Could that make a difference in the relationship you have with your boss? I believe it could make a profound impact on the spread of the gospel, based on the Titus 2 passage, cited previously.

An acquaintance of ours, a businessman in Ecuador, recently made an interesting suggestion along these lines. He said he believed that Christianity overwhelmed the Roman Empire, not so much by the preaching of the great apostles and evangelists such as Paul, Peter, or Philip, but by the work ethic of its many Christian slaves, who overwhelmed their Roman masters by their Christlike attitudes and actions on the job.

This is quite possibly true, because easily half of the population at that time were slaves; and the gospel of Christ flourished among them, as the many passages addressed to them in the New Testament attest.

What could happen today if the many employees who call themselves Christians lived a distinctive, Christlike lifestyle on the job? Might it overwhelm their employers, who are dying to see workers committed to excellence and high productivity? It would if those outstanding qualities were shown to be the result of Christ in the lives of the workers.

YOUR MARRIAGE

Ephesians 5:22-33 likens the relationship between a husband and a wife to the union between Christ and the Church. The picture is one of intimacy and communion, loyalty and mutual submission. From this standpoint, it's not enough for Christians to simply keep their marriages together, but to arrange their lives such that they grow together. That's God's ideal.

Of course, we live in a very complex world, a world much different from both the Old and New Testament cultures. But God's idea and ideals for marriage have not changed. He still wants couples to grow together. That's a value worth holding onto.

However, one of the greatest threats to your marriage that you may ever encounter is the subtle pressure to succeed. As we've seen, our culture's picture of success is usually painted in terms of a career. And it's not unusual for both spouses to be in the work world. This can be good for your finances, but devastating to your marriage. The demands and opportunities of your job(s) can slowly pull you apart. It's a situation that Sheldon Vanauken aptly described as "creeping separateness."

In *How to Balance Competing Time Demands*, Bill and I suggest a number of practical steps you and your spouse can take to avoid growing apart. Two points are worth emphasizing to encourage you to grow together. First, you must commit yourself to building a godly marriage, even if it means sacrificing certain achievements in your career.

That flies in the face of accepted practice in America

today. On every hand, marriages are flying apart because they have become a professional liability. That's precisely why you must determine to make yours work as best you can. If that means a certain loss of income, if it hinders your progress up the career ladder, if it puts you at a competitive disadvantage, so be it. Your commitment must lie with succeeding in your marriage more than succeeding in your career.

That commitment must be acted upon. So a second point to suggest is that you and your spouse find at *least* one evening (or an equivalent period of time) each week just to be together—not to do chores, not to go shopping, not to go to a movie. Just to be together—to talk to each other, to share each other's thoughts and feelings, to become friends rather than strangers.

If you want to build a marriage that survives a career, start by setting this book down. Get out your scheduling book or calendar, and work out a time with your spouse when the two of you can just be together.

YOUR FAMILY

Another category of relationships that God places great emphasis on has to do with your family. If you're a parent, the same forces that can destroy your marriage can also destroy your children. There's no way around the fact that your children need your acceptance, companionship, model, counsel, discipline, wisdom . . . and time!

Two suggestions that are *similar* to those just mentioned are: (1) commit yourself to meeting the need your children have for a parent and not just your need for career success; and (2) schedule special time with *each* of your kids—just the two of you—at least once each week.

If possible, do something you'll both enjoy.

I have yet to hear about a man or woman on his or her death bed who has said with regret, "I wish I'd spent more time at work!" But I sure know plenty of folks who already feel incredible remorse that they have paid for their very successful careers by mortgaging their children. That's a deal in which everyone loses. Don't lose your kids through misplaced priorities!

Let me add that family responsibilities don't end with your kids. Biblically, each of us has a continuing responsibility to our other family members, especially our parents, as long as they are alive. Practically speaking, how often do you talk with your parents? How often do you see them? Are they adequately provided for? Are you continuing to cultivate a relationship with them?

One of the great tragedies of our success-driven culture is the breakdown of family relationships. We have emphasized material gain and social status at the expense of the people closest to us. If God measures our lives by the quality of our relationships, then we as Christians, of all people, should excel at caring for those in our families.

CHAPTER THIRTEEN

A Value on Serving God

Have you ever noticed how in any group of people, there's always an "in" crowd, and then there's everyone else? This is certainly the case in most workplaces. Quite apart from rank on the organizational chart, most organizations have a sort of informal confederation of insiders, sometimes several of these groups.

The insiders all share a certain view of "the way things *really* are around here!" They have jokes in common, certain phrases and code words, even special gestures and looks that represent shared memories and understanding. The funny thing is, you're never quite asked to be in such a group, never directly. Yet after you've been subtly tested and tried, one day you find yourself one of "us," as opposed to being one of "them."

Groups of insiders are not necessarily bad. They are really quite normal and unavoidable. Nor is the feeling of belonging to such an exclusive cadre wrong in itself. But what can be very dangerous is the *desire* to get in on the inside. That ambition can lead a person to do some very bad things.

Marcy illustrates this well. She worked at a consulting firm in New England. In her segment of the company, an insiders' group formed when two new people were hired. They had gone to graduate school together and already had a lot in common. Once in the firm, they met several of Marcy's friends with whom they seemed to click.

Within a matter of weeks, this group began to get together after work every day. They often ate lunch together, and some even worked out together at a fitness club. This became more than just a network of friends and coworkers; it became an insiders' group.

And Marcy was left out. Somehow she didn't quite "make the team." Sometimes she tagged along for after-hours refreshments, or invited her friends and some of the new crowd over for dinner. But even then, she realized that a chemistry was at play among them that did not include her. She didn't understand the stories and jokes, she often felt uninformed about the topics of discussion, and she could tell that a lot of things were going on among the group when she was not around—things to which she was not invited.

Naturally, Marcy felt an increasing sense of loneliness and isolation, and the unique terror of being left out. She reacted by fighting back. She began to inflate her own work and achievements far beyond their real worth to the company. At the same time, she often disparaged projects that some of the insiders worked on, criticizing their performance and trying to diminish their value to the company. Her criticisms took on an increasingly personal tone, and she spiced her comments with tidbits of private information about the flaws of people in the group. In the end, she even resorted to sabotaging some of their work. She "accidentally" lost data important to them, detoured reports they needed, "forgot" to relay messages to them, and even altered crucial numbers.

Marcy desperately wanted to belong, to be accepted—so desperately that she let herself be overcome by bitterness when she felt rejected. That was so unfortunate. The desire for the approval of others was a strong force for her, as it is for many of us. It's a major factor that drives many people in our culture in their pursuit of success.

Of course, it's natural for us to be concerned with what our peer group thinks of us. We'd all like to enjoy the approval of others. Some are more prone to depend on that than others. It's interesting that God regards such approval as a little fish. What others think of us doesn't count for much in His estimation.

It's funny, though, what we'll do to gain that acceptance. Consider our purchases, for instance. Someone has perceptively said that most of us buy things we don't need with money we don't have to impress people we don't know or don't like!

What a bold challenge, then, we find in Isaiah 2:22:

Stop regarding man, whose breath of life is in his nostrils; for why should he be esteemed?

Pursuing image and status in order to impress others and win their esteem is a tiny fish in a biblical view of success. As God redirects your values, you'll increasingly develop *a nonchalance about the approval of others, but a deep concern with faithfully serving God at work.* It's a redirection in who you're trying to please.

Stop for a moment and ask yourself: what would I do differently in my work if Jesus Christ were my boss? If

He were my supervisor, the one handing out my assignments and reviewing my performance, how would that change the way I do my job?

If Jesus were there in person, would it affect your performance? Would you be more productive? Would you look for ways to get the job done faster, with less expense, and even ahead of schedule? How would that affect your relationships on the job? Would your speech and language change? Would your behavior toward the opposite sex change? Would it affect the way you resolve conflicts? What about the politics and gamesmanship that so often go on? Would it make you more sensitive to people, more compassionate?

I don't know how you respond to these kinds of questions, but the fact is, Jesus *is* your ultimate Boss. He has very definite expectations for you as you carry out your job. Notice Ephesians 6:5:

> Slaves, be obedient to those who are your masters according to the flesh, with fear and trembling, in the sincerity of your heart, as to Christ.

Paul addresses himself to slaves in this context. Sometimes you may feel like a slave at your job. But these people were real slaves—captured peoples made to serve their Roman-world conquerors. They carried out the menial tasks; though, as we have seen in the parable of the talents, some assumed great responsibility and management.

Paul tells these workers that they should work for their Ephesian masters as if those masters were Jesus Christ. In fact, he tells them, to work "with fear and trembling, in the sincerity of your heart." If you're familiar with the Bible, you may recognize that these words are almost always used with reference to a person's relationship to God. People are to "fear" God—not to be afraid of Him, but to respect Him, to worship Him, to hold Him in esteem. But here Paul says we are to offer that same respect to our earthly employers.

The reason is that behind them stands Jesus Christ. He is our ultimate Boss. The way we respond to our earthly employers is really the way in which we're responding to Christ's lordship over our li ves. When we go to work, we should obey our bosses because we consciously recognize that our ultimate Boss is Christ.

This can have a profound impact on the way you see your work and the way you approach it. Suppose that as you put on your tie or your makeup each morning, you looked at yourself in the mirror and said, "Today I'm going to work to serve and honor and please Jesus Christ!" What a difference that could make. In the first place, doing that affirms the dignity and the high calling of your work. If Jesus is your Boss, then your work *matters* to God!

In addition, recognizing Jesus as your Boss could dramatically affect your attitude on the job. Look at what Paul went on to say (5:6): "Not by way of eyeservice, as men-pleasers, but as slaves of Christ, doing the will of God from the heart."

It's a sad reality of life that many people work hard only when the boss is watching them. In fact, about forty percent of American workers report that they only do just enough work to keep their jobs. That's not serving Christ, "doing the will of God from the heart"; that's working "by way of eyeservice, as men-pleasers."

One of the more humorous events I observed in the Air Force was inspection day. Headquarters would send a team of inspectors to our base to ensure that everything and everybody was up to standard.

We wise guys in the flight room always said that on these inspection days we heard the two biggest lies ever told in the Air Force. First, the commander of the inspection team would step off the plane to greet the wing commander of the base, and he'd always say, "Hello, we're here to help you." (The first biggest lie!) Then the wing commander would respond, "Thank you, sir, we're glad you're here!" (The second.)

It was funny to watch the way everybody went into crisis mode a few weeks before the arrival of an inspection team. All the grass got clipped; the mess hall floor got waxed; the buildings got scrubbed; hair cuts became much shorter; boots would get a double shine—all to put our best face on for the brass. Of course, as soon as their plane left, things would start heading back downhill!

The point is, we diligently prepared for an inspection team, the "eyes" of the bosses in Washington; but once they were gone, we reverted to less careful habits. But the Ephesians passage instructs us that serving God at work is not at all like that. We're not to do our work well only when the boss or others have their eyes on us, to gain their approval. Instead, we're to serve diligently and faithfully no matter who is or isn't watching. Ultimately, we're serving Christ. Paul goes on (5:7-8):

> With good will render service, as to the Lord, and not to men, knowing that whatever good thing each one does, this he will receive back from the Lord, whether slave or free.

Christ *always* has His eye on us. In the end, He'll evaluate our work when we stand before Him someday. What will He say of you? How will your final performance review read? Like the first two managers in the parable of the talents, will you merit a "promotion"? Will He say, "Well done"? Or, will you be evaluated like the third slave as wicked and lazy? The outcome will depend in part on the extent to which you cultivate a nonchalance about the approval of others, but a *deep concern* with serving God.

Let me offer one practical means by which you can get started toward that goal. I suggest that you write a one-page *career manifesto*. A career manifesto is simply a purpose statement of your commitment to serve Jesus Christ in your job, followed by several practical ways of what that might look like for you.

For instance, suppose you're a plumber. We need plumbers with a Christlike work ethic. It's a vital occupation that is usually thankless. A career manifesto for a plumber might start with a brief statement of intention: "As a plumber, my purpose is to faithfully serve Jesus Christ by repairing and maintaining the water and sewage facilities of people in my community." Then you might draw out a brief picture of what that would look like in practical terms:

- •I will complete my jobs as efficiently as I can and on time.
- •I will charge a fair price for my services and materials.
- •I will charge only for work that I actually perform, and only do work that is actually needed.
- •I will guarantee my work appropriately, and correct mistakes at my own expense.
- •I will look for opportunities to explain to my customers and employees or coworkers that I want to do my best work because my ultimate

Boss is Jesus Christ.
•I will maintain my truck and equipment in a safe
condition in accordance with the law and the
standards of my industry.

To be sure, if you're actually a plumber, you may
have different suggestions than these and a greater
number. But the point is to be plain and practical about
what it would look like to serve Christ as a plumber.

I strongly urge you, no matter what your job is—
teacher, insurance agent, software programmer, government employee, career homemaker, rocket scientist,
minister—sit down right now and write out a brief career
manifesto. You'll be amazed at how helpful that can be
in developing a deep concern for serving Christ where
you work.

A biblical view of success will have a strong impact
on your values the longer you pursue it. As we've seen, it
will foster:

1. A nonchalance about professional recognition,
but a deep concern for integrity.
2. A nonchalance about ladders and titles, but a
deep concern with character growth.
3. A nonchalance about financial status, but a deep
concern for relationships.
4. A nonchalance about the approval of others, but
a deep concern with faithfully serving God at
work.

There is a third major area in which God's view of
success will affect life—the critical area of decision making. Look with me now at a number of practical ways a
biblical view of success affects your decisions.

New Ways of Making Decisions

Every day, each of us makes dozens of choices, and over a year's time, we make thousands, perhaps tens of thousands of decisions. Many are relatively insignificant: Where should we buy gas? Do we want ham-and-swiss or tuna-on-rye? Which suit or skirt should we wear?

But many choices are far more significant, because they affect not only our own lives but also the lives of many other people.

Several decades ago, a black father took his son to a shoe store in Atlanta. It was a period of extreme segregation and racial prejudice. Although the store was empty, the white salesclerk said, "If you'll move to the back, I'll be glad to help you."

But the father wouldn't tolerate this. "You'll wait on us here," he said, "or we won't buy any shoes." The clerk replied that he couldn't do that, whereupon the father took his son by the hand and left the store.

Outside, he explained his behavior to his son: "I don't care how long I have to live with this thing, I'll never accept it. I'll fight it till I die. Nobody can make a slave out of you if you don't think like a slave."

A minor incident in the long and painful struggle by America's blacks for equality and justice? Not when you learn that the black man was the father of Martin Luther King, Jr. The boy never forgot that incident; it was formative in his outlook. Through his son, Daddy King's simple but firm decision had an extremely powerful impact on generations of Americans.

Sometimes choices can cause catastrophe. One has only to think of the disaster that befell the space shuttle *Challenger*. Despite repeated warnings from lower level technicians and engineers, the decision was made to launch. When the rocket booster's infamous O-rings failed, seven astronauts perished, and a billion-dollar spacecraft disintegrated before America's eyes. Seven sets of families were left to grieve over their losses. Untold billions were spent to correct that problem. The shuttle program was severely delayed. Several careers were ruined.

Consider the savings and loan crisis that is growing like a towering, ugly thundercloud every day as I write this book. Examiners believe that one of the key factors creating the turmoil was fraud, greed, and criminal mismanagement by a small minority of S&L insiders. Their decisions to arrange illegal loans and to squander assets on lavish parties, private jets, and exotic getaways created a wreck that will likely cost American taxpayers between $100 billion and $150 billion. But the toll on the communities and regions in which these institutions failed is incalculable. Many businesses and individuals may never fully recover from the damage done.

Seen in this light, our choices and how we make them take on a dramatic importance. We need to know, as we consider the decision-making process, that nearly all decisions are value-driven. In other words, we'll always make our choices based on what matters most to us, what we really care about. Our values are the backbone on which all our decisions rest.

In the illustrations cited, for instance: Daddy King chose to leave the store rather than cooperate with a segregationist policy, because he valued his freedom, his equality, and his dignity. Those who chose to disregard clear warnings against the ability of the O-rings to withstand extreme cold apparently valued the timeframe under which NASA and its various contractors were working. The handful of savings and loan principals who chose to mishandle their responsibilities must have valued the status and prestige of being able to throw a lot of money around.

Our decisions, especially the major ones, will inevitably be value-driven. That's why it's so critical that our values be in line with God's values, as we saw in the last four chapters. Unfortunately, many people in our culture rush headlong in a furious pursuit of career success, making choices driven by ungodly values. These choices are having and will have a devastating effect on their marriages and children, on their coworkers and customers, on their communities, and on our society as a whole.

That's not what you want. You want a life built on wise choices, choices informed by a godly view of success. In the next three chapters, we'll see how that view might affect your decisions in three areas: your integrity, your schedule, and the use of your money.

CHAPTER FOURTEEN

Decisions About Integrity

Have you ever needed to lose some weight? I find that I go through a cycle every year where I get myself in decent shape over the summer, but then the fall comes, which is always a hectic time, and my exercise starts slacking off. Then the holidays roll around, and Jan and I get invited to countless parties where the food is inevitably too good to pass up. About mid-January, my friends are seeing more of me than they ought to! About that time, I usually decide to go on a diet.

Having been down this road a number of times, I've learned a crucial lesson about dieting: You have to decide ahead of time what you can and can't eat. Apart from that, you'll never succeed. If you don't have a plan, and instead wait until you're at the table to decide what to eat, you'll always overeat. When the cheesecake or the chocolate suicide is staring you in the face, you'll never be able to say no if you haven't said no before you sit down.

When it comes to the ethical decisions we all have to make, this same principle of dieting comes into play.

Decisions that affect our integrity are best made ahead of time—before we're in a situation that asks us to compromise. Let me suggest three decisions you'll want to make ahead of time, before you ever get to work.

DECIDE TO TELL THE TRUTH

The first decision sounds so simple and obvious that it hardly seems worth mentioning. But while deciding to tell the truth sounds easy, there's a tremendous temptation in the workplace each day to tell little white lies. Of course, little white lies are neither little nor white. But regardless, deception is a *major* temptation for most of us in today's work world.

Imagine, for instance, that you're at your desk when your phone rings. You answer, and at the other end is a very angry customer. He wants to know where his shipment is—the one you promised to have to him by now. He doesn't have it yet, he needs it, and he's furious.

Naturally, you're shocked to suddenly realize you never sent his shipment. But you want to save face; you don't want to admit that you botched the order. So what do you do? It's easy, too easy at that point, to lie—to say to the customer that you can't imagine why it isn't there yet. Why, it's already been shipped, you tell him. Is he certain it's not sitting somewhere in his receiving department? Well, if it's not there today, surely he should be getting it tomorrow! Somehow you stave him off and hang up. Then you dial Federal Express!

In the heat of battle it's all too easy to compromise. That's why a biblical view of success encourages you to decide ahead of time to tell the truth, even if it means losing face. Honesty pleases God, and pleasing God is what true success is all about. Notice Proverbs 12:22:

Lying lips are an abomination to the LORD,
But those who deal faithfully are His delight.

There are not a lot of things in Scripture called an "abomination," but lying lips are. God hates lies. All lies. That's why it's better to tell a customer that you failed, made a mistake, and will make amends, than to deceive him to save face. After all, you want God to delight in you, as the verse explains.

It is so crucial that you decide *ahead of time* that you're firmly committed to telling the truth—no matter what.

A real estate developer was in a partnership with two other men. They were putting up a project of condominiums. The institution providing the financing had arranged to give them money in three phases. As the first phase was completed and leased out, a loan for the second phase would be given. When that was completed and leased out, money for the third phase would be given.

Phase one was complete and leased out. Phase two was nearly complete, but it was far from completely leased. However, two of the partners were eager to get going on the third phase, which would be the most lucrative part of the project.

The partners arranged to meet with the loan officer. As they were waiting outside his office, one man asked his two partners how they expected to get financing for the third phase when the terms for the second had not yet been met. The two partners looked at each other and smiled. "Don't worry," they said, "we've written up contracts with our relatives and friends. As soon as we get the money for phase three, we'll tear up those agreements."

At that very moment, the loan officer came out and

said, "Gentlemen, welcome. Won't you please step into my office."

What would you do in a situation like that? Think of all that's on the line! Unless you've decided ahead of time that honesty is your rule, you'll find it very easy to compromise yourself.

DECIDE TO FOLLOW YOUR CONSCIENCE

Your conscience is a God-given ability to detect right from wrong—an ability that often guides us in our moral choices—especially in areas where the Scriptures do not give black-and-white instructions.

Hebrews 5:14 speaks of the mature believer as having his senses trained to discern good and evil. The passage is talking about the conscience. Over time, as we feed on God's Word and as we go through various situations, we develop an inner sense about what is right and wrong. This is our conscience. It acts like a moral compass or gyroscope, keeping us on a godly course. It allows us to navigate through the ninety-nine shades of gray that confront us in ethical choices.

We have an excellent illustration of this faculty at work in the biblical story of Daniel. He was taken by the Babylonians from his home in Palestine and put into a special training program under the king's chief official (Daniel 1:1-8). Immediately Daniel was confronted with a problem, for the king ordered that the youths in the program be given special food. The Bible doesn't tell us why Daniel found this food to be morally objectionable, but it says he "made up his mind that he would not defile himself with the king's choice food" (verse 8). Notice how his conscience helped him make a decision. If you investigate the context and the history of Daniel, you'll see that he had made up his mind to obey his godly conscience before he ever left Judaea.

First Peter 3:15-16 puts all of this together for us:

> But sanctify Christ as Lord in your hearts, always being ready to make a defense to every one who asks you to give an account for the hope that is in you, yet with gentleness and reverence; and keep a good conscience so that in the thing in which you are slandered, those who revile your good behavior in Christ may be put to shame.

Notice the connection between keeping a good conscience and making Christ the Lord of your life. That's something you must do before you face a troubling situation. You must prepare yourself to hold onto your convictions before you ever face a temptation (see also Ephesians 6:14, 1 Peter 1:13).

Ed is a good illustration of this. He was a lawyer in a large, prestigious law firm. He was young and sharp, with bright prospects. He was also a person committed to Christ. Over time, he began to feel increasing pressure from the senior partners and other lawyers in the firm to put in more hours—that is, to put in more billable hours. At first they wanted him to stay late, then they wanted his evenings; then they asked for his weekends.

As the demands increased, however, Ed's conscience began to bother him. He knew that his family would have to make sacrifices if he was going to be a lawyer, but he felt that the hours he was being asked to work made those sacrifices too great. Ed finally drew the line and informed the firm of his limits. In time, it became apparent that his limits were unacceptable to the firm. So he eventually left for a position at a much smaller, less demanding law practice.

Did Ed's decision to follow his conscience cost him in terms of his career advancement? Sure it did. But he had already decided to pursue biblical success. For him, in this situation, that meant leaving a prestigious, high-paying law firm. But he would say it was a small price to pay to do what was right for his family. God will reward him for that. Jesus promised in John 12:26: "If anyone serves Me . . . the Father will honor him."

DECIDE TO FULFILL YOUR WORD

A final decision you should make ahead of time is that you're going to keep your word no matter what. This kind of faithfulness and reliability is quickly becoming unknown in our society. Instead, people make contingency commitments—they'll do what they said they'd do *unless* a better deal comes along.

A certain investor, for example, signed an agreement to buy an apartment building from an elderly widow. This woman had held onto the property long after her husband's death, planning to sell it and use the profit for her retirement. The day of the closing came and the woman gathered with her lawyer and the lawyers for the investor. In he walked, stunning everyone by announcing, "I've changed my mind. I've found something else I'd rather invest in. You can sue me if you want." And he walked out.

That's a contingency commitment: I'll fulfill my word unless something better comes along. The real tragedy of the story was that this man enjoyed a high profile in the community as a believer, the sort of person every ministry wanted on its board. Can you imagine the disrepute that such a flip-flop created for the cause of

Christ in that community?

Unlike this investor, the person who pursues true success determines to keep his or her word no matter what. This quality of faithfulness is one of the fruits of the Spirit mentioned in Galatians 5:22-23, and it's a sign that Christ is in control of a person's life.

Earlier in the book we looked at Psalm 15—a passage that describes the sort of person who enjoys a close, intimate relationship with God. Recall that integrity was the big fish in that passage. Part of integrity is this matter of fulfilling one's word. In the latter part of verse 4 we read, "He swears to his own hurt, and does not change." In other words, integrity means that we follow through on our commitments, even when it's inconvenient, even when it costs. We don't make commitments easily, and we don't take them lightly when we make them.

Two friends of mine provide an excellent illustration of this. They owned an extremely profitable business. They put it up for sale, and gave their word that, pending a few details, they would sell to a particular buyer. They made this commitment on a Friday. However, over the weekend they received another offer that would have netted them an enormously higher profit.

Unsure of what they should do, they spent the rest of the weekend praying with their wives. By Sunday night they all agreed that their word must be their bond. On Monday morning, they called the second buyer and turned down his better offer. Unlike the investor in the incident with the elderly woman, they said "no" to many dollars on the basis that they had to fulfill their word.

God honors people who live this way. Psalm 15:5 promises, "He who does these things will never be shaken." If you want the security of living with God's approval, with His smile upon your life, then I urge you to make these important decisions that will affect your integrity:

- •Decide to tell the truth.
- •Decide to follow your conscience.
- •Decide to fulfill your word.
- •Decide that these will be your values—before you're ever asked to compromise.

CHAPTER FIFTEEN

Decisions About Your Time

Have you ever heard of Tim Hansel's paperback *When I Relax I Feel Guilty*? I came across it several years ago and it's been a real help. I tend to be one of the "weary servants of the impossible" to whom Tim wrote. And yes, I have a hard time relaxing—purposing to have no purpose.

In his book, Hansel cited Leslie Flynn, who once asked, "What would you do if every morning without fail your bank called to say that 86,400 pennies had been credited to your account overnight?" By the way, no balance could be carried over to the next day; whatever was not spent could not be saved. Would you use every penny every day? You bet!

Well, that's exactly the situation with our time. Every night at the stroke of midnight, 86,400 seconds are deposited in our account. We must use 'em or lose 'em. We can't really save time; we can only spend it. How do you spend yours?

Your answer to that question is one of the most far-reaching decisions you can make. And you make it every day. Are you choosing wisely? Why is it that two people can have exactly the same amount of time—86,400 seconds each day—and yet one lives life to the full, while the other languishes in boredom, wasted time, and wasted efforts?

Think back to the parable of the talents. Remember that the wealthy owner gave various measures of his treasure to each of three slaves to use for business while he was gone. The two who invested wisely received praise when the master returned, but the third slave was denounced as wicked and lazy for neglecting his responsibilities.

In discussing that parable, I said that it showed how true success before God means faithfully pleasing Him with the resources and responsibilities He's given us. Time is one of the most valuable of those resources. How we use our time—our 86,400 seconds each day—says a lot about how faithful we're trying to be.

As you make time commitments and evaluate your schedule, I urge you to consider three important principles.

GOD WANTS YOU TO BE WISE
ABOUT YOUR USE OF TIME

Every careerist I've ever met has an agenda. Perhaps you do. Perhaps your long-range objective is to own your own company, or maybe to be CEO of a corporation. Maybe it's to be a millionaire by a specific year. Maybe it's a modest goal of retiring comfortably at a certain age. Whatever your plan, you're probably very busy as you carry it out.

Suppose, however, you were stuck in a holding pattern where objectives seemed pointless. Many people facing long terms in prison feel that way. Some who are laid up with permanent disabilities or health conditions feel that way.

Moses felt that way. He had grown up in Egypt, tended sheep in Midian, returned in the power of God to lead the Hebrews out of Egypt, led them all the way across the Sinai Peninsula to the Promised Land—the Land of Canaan—only to be turned back by the people's unbelief at Kadesh Barnea (Numbers 13–14).

For the next forty years, Moses and the Israelites wandered back and forth across the Sinai. They were in a holding pattern. And do you know what they were waiting for? They were waiting for people to die! God had said that until all the "numbered men" twenty years of age and up had died off Israel would not enter the land.

Day after day, year after year, Moses watched as one by one the numbered men died, leaving corpses scattered in the desert. What a depressing existence! Forty years of life going nowhere, wandering around, waiting for people to die!

It was from this backdrop that Moses composed Psalm 90. Not surprisingly, it speaks of the eternity of God and the temporary, fleeting appearance of mankind. Lodged strategically in this psalm is a curious request—a prayer addressed to God. But like so many prayers, it is a bit of a sermon to the people listening. Verse 12 asks,

> So teach us to number our days,
> That we may present to Thee a heart of wisdom.

Teach us to number our days. Moses had forty years to do that—forty years in the desert with no place to go and nothing to accomplish. How about you? Have you learned to number your days? If you're driven by career success—whatever that looks like for you—I suspect you may be so busy that the only thought you've given to "your days" has been a conversation with an insurance agent!

But Moses is telling us that our time is a gift, a resource from God. He wants us to be wise in how we use it. Even if you're fit and trim at thirty, in all likelihood, you don't even have 20,000 days left to live! (As I pointed out earlier, on any given day you have only 86,400 seconds. Use 'em or lose 'em!) How are you using yours?

In Ephesians 5, Paul writes from a considerably brighter outlook than Moses. Yet he sounds very similar (verses 15-16):

> Therefore be careful how you walk, not as unwise men, but as wise, making the most of your time, because the days are evil.

Making the most of your time. Numbering your days. God wants us to take time seriously, to use it wisely. It's a valuable, nonrenewable resource to be used carefully. How can we do that? How can we "walk, not as unwise men, but as wise"? Let's find out by looking at two more considerations that should guide your use of time.

YOU NEED TO BALANCE YOUR RESPONSIBILITIES

If you've been around Christians for any length of time, you've probably heard a listing of priorities presented that goes something like this: In your life you need to put

God first, family second, church third, and so on. The "and so on" varies and usually gets pretty vague; but those first three often seem to be set in stone: God first, family second, church third.

There is some value to this hierarchy. For instance, if you're forced to choose between keeping your marriage together or moving ahead in your career, biblically I think you'd have to choose in favor of your marriage.

However, I don't find that hierarchy to be very helpful for planning my commitments; nor do I find it to be especially biblical. It's not very helpful because it's rare that a person faces extreme, either/or choices between God and family, or family and career, or God and career, or whatever. Most of the choices we face are not either/or but both/and: We want to build a good marriage *and* do excellent work in our jobs; we want to spend time with our kids *and* have valuable fellowship with other Christians; we want to spend time alone with God *and* stay up on developments in our government and communities. On the whole, living life doesn't require a hierarchy of priorities, but rather a balance among our commitments.

Perhaps that's why the Bible doesn't really teach a hierarchy. God is not at the top of any list: He's the Lord over *all* of life (Colossians 3:17). Whatever we do, we should do it to the glory of God. Remember, there is no dichotomy between the sacred and the secular taught in Scripture.

What we do find in Scripture is that God desires a measure of faithfulness in five broad categories of life: our personal and spiritual life; our family; our work; our church; and our community. God has given us responsibilities in each of these areas. We must balance our use of time in carrying out these responsibilities.

Let me mention a very practical principle regarding balanced responsibilities: Whenever you add something to your schedule, you must subtract something somewhere else to maintain balance. Otherwise you'll quickly become overcommitted—and weary!

So, for example, if your son's soccer league asks you to coach, you may decide to say yes. But in doing so, you need to ask yourself: What other commitment can I drop in order to take this one on? Don't just let demands and responsibilities pile up without sloughing off some of them. If you're overcommitted, you'll quickly lose perspective, and you'll have a hard time being faithful to God in all five of the areas mentioned.

Here is a related principle to this balance of responsibilities.

YOU NEED TO GUARD YOUR USE OF EMOTIONAL ENERGY

A world-renowned management expert says that American business today creates and rewards the six-meter high-jumper. Have you ever seen someone who could jump six meters high? That's nearly twenty feet! Is that possible?

What this expert is facetiously suggesting is that in an age of specialization and sub-specialization and super-specialization, people figure out what they can do unusually well, and then they get a job doing that one thing over and over and over again. If a guy can jump six meters high, he's paid to do that. He does that one thing well, extraordinarily well. But that's *all* he can do! In fact, that's *all* he's paid to do. As a result, he tends to become terribly narrow and one-dimensional. Aside from high jumping, he really has little to offer and little to pursue.

For many of us this manifests itself in the extreme amount of emotional energy we put into our work. Work not only dominates our time, it dominates our emotional life. Ask something about our work, and we light up like a Christmas tree. Any other subject, though, and we may lose interest quickly.

We'll put enormous creative energy and effort into planning a project at work and getting it done. We'll sacrifice sleep, meals, days off—whatever it takes as we become absorbed in the task. But when it comes to planning a simple outing with the family, or helping our spouse work through a problem, or giving forethought to our spiritual objectives over the coming months, we suddenly feel very tired and disinterested. It's apparent that tasks like these cannot seem to capture the same attention and energy as our work. In short, work dominates our emotional energy.

When we consider a biblical view of work and life, we find that work is only one of five areas that must be kept in perspective. It's not just our allocation of time that must be balanced; it's our allocation of emotional energy as well.

If I'm going to be faithful to God in, say, my responsibility to my kids, then I have to put as much effort into nurturing and cultivating those relationships as I would into anything I do at Career Impact Ministries.

Consider, for example, how much energy and planning I have to give to CIM's quarterly board meetings. I help set the agenda. I go through several planning meetings with staff and board members. I spend considerable time in prayer about each meeting. Then I have to attend and make my contribution to the discussion. I have to be sensitive to each of the comments offered by the board members, considering their implications and impact. After the meeting, I have to debrief and then carry out whatever assignments I've been given. In short, I expend enormous energy and effort to make each board meeting a useful exercise.

But I've discovered that if I'm to be faithful to God as a father, I have to put forth similar effort in the things I do with my kids. Granted, my kids are a relationship—not a task, not a project—so the dynamics are different. But the emotional commitment must *not* be different! If I'm going to do something with my kids, I need to deliberately think through that activity and what it will take to make it successful. I need to coordinate my schedule with theirs and make sure that the activities are something worth doing. I may have to get some things ready—like fix a bike, buy a new net for the basketball hoop, gas up the car, or make reservations.

As we do the activity, I need to concentrate on my kids and their needs and interests—not on a problem or idea at work. I need to listen to what they say and respond intelligently and appropriately to their questions. Afterwards, I probably need to "debrief" with them, reflecting on what we've done and anything we may have learned or anything we especially enjoyed about the time. Maybe I need to get pictures developed, or help them tell their mom about their adventures, or arrange for a rain check on something we didn't get to do.

In short, I have to exert a lot of energy and emotion as I relate to my kids—just as I exert energy and emotion for things at CIM. You know what? That's hard work; it takes a *lot* of energy!

So if I pour all of my energy into my job and leave none of it for my children, then I won't be able to do my job of fathering very well at all. In fact, I'll tend to see my kids as nothing but a distraction to my work!

I don't think that would be acceptable to God. True success means faithfully pleasing Him in *all* of my responsibilities—certainly my kids are one of the most important. Work is important, too; so are many other things. That's why I have to guard how I use my emotional energy. I have to balance it out, so that I have adequate reserves for each area.

When I stand before God someday, I don't believe He's going to be impressed if the only thing I've done with my life is jump six meters high at CIM. Not when He's assigned me many other events, too. In order to "walk, not as an unwise man, but as wise," I must accept limits on my career aspirations and plans, in order to focus on additional roles and responsibilities.

As you plan your day-to-day activities, I encourage you to review the resources and assignments God has given you in each of five areas: your personal and spiritual life, your family, your work, your church, and your community. Are you being faithful to God in each area? Where does each one fit in your schedule? How much emotional energy are you devoting to each? Remember that your use of time reflects your values. Make sure your calendar reflects a commitment to true success!

CHAPTER SIXTEEN

Decisions About Your Money

Have you ever been in such dire straits financially that you've had to consult a financial counselor? Perhaps you've over-extended yourself, racked up too many credit purchases, failed to stay within your budget, or made poor investments. My friends in the financial planning and consulting field tell me some incredible stories about how deep in the hole people sometimes get themselves.

One of the things they inevitably point out is how a person's spending habits and priorities are like a huge bay window that looks directly in upon their values. People express what matters to them by how they handle their money. And when you look in on many people in our culture, you immediately discover how the image of success matters more than anything else. You can see it in their checkbooks, even more on the credit histories. Money is a way to keep score, to tell who is really succeeding and who is not.

Suppose I had your checkbook and charge slips in front of me. What would they reveal about your values and priorities? If you want them to reflect a godly view of success, then I encourage you to keep three principles in mind as you make financial decisions (i.e., *every* time you write a check).

YOUR MONEY, LIKE YOUR TIME, IS A VALUABLE RESOURCE FROM GOD

Money has gotten very bad press over the centuries in most Christian teaching. (At least it did until Prosperity Theology came along.) In the main, money has been harshly condemned. In fact, some people have gone so far as to say that money is inherently evil, intrinsically corrupting; that it is an idol just like Baal or the other pagan deities condemned in Scripture.

Money has traditionally been disparaged among Christians precisely because it's been exalted by most cultures. Certainly in our own day, the color of green is very much in vogue. Money is power, money is freedom, money is security.

Given these polar extremes, it's no wonder that many of us feel a lot of confusion over exactly how God sees money. We hear a sermon that says He's down on money, but then a plate is passed to collect some of it. Often the sermon is delivered in a multimillion-dollar facility, requiring enormous sums of money to heat and cool and staff. Is God really down on money?

Let's let Jesus speak for Himself. In Matthew 6:19-21, He expresses Himself clearly in this familiar passage:

> "Do not lay up for yourselves treasures upon earth, where moth and rust destroy, and where thieves break in and steal. But lay up for your-

selves treasures in heaven, where neither moth
nor rust destroys, and where thieves do not break
in or steal; for where your treasure is, there will
your heart be also."

It would appear that Jesus is quite concerned about
our use of money, though notice He doesn't condemn it
outright. What he specifically warns us *not* to do is "lay
up for ourselves treasures upon earth." Does this mean
to not have a savings account or any investments? (Given
the recent catastrophes in the banking and savings and
loan industries and the precarious behavior of the stock
market, that may be worth considering!)

The key to understanding Jesus' teaching is that last
line: where our treasure is, there will our heart be also.
The way we handle money reflects our "heart," our basic
values. As I said before, it's like a bay window that looks
in on our lives. People who put all their money into
earth-bound, time-bound things show that they are
earth-bound, time-bound people. They are literally
spending as if there is no tomorrow!

But there *is* a tomorrow! There is a day when we will
be with God. How we use the money we have *now* says
everything about whether that matters to us. If our
perspective on money is wrong, it's because our perspective on the rest of life and eternity is wrong as well. This
passage doesn't end here. Though it's rarely included,
Jesus goes on (6:22-23):

"The lamp of the body is the eye; if therefore your
eye is clear, your whole body will be full of light.
But if your eye is bad, your whole body will be
full of darkness. If therefore the light that is in you
is darkness, how great is the darkness!"

Jesus uses the eye to illustrate His point. You're able to read the words on this page because your eye can see them. Your eye is "clear." It enables light to enter your body. But suppose you were blind. You would be unable to read or to see. In that sense, your world would be "dark." You would be unaware of the way things are visually.

When it comes to money, Jesus is saying, there are a lot of blind people wandering around who don't see beyond this present life—people who don't have the big picture. In fact, in our culture there are a great many blind leading the blind!

Are you financially blind? You are if God is not the Master of your finances. Financial blindness has nothing to do with whether you can read a spreadsheet, pick winning stocks, or even balance your checkbook. Jesus says you are blind if you're handling your money as if God doesn't exist or doesn't matter. He clinches it when He adds this famous statement (6:24):

> "No one can serve two masters; for either he will hate the one and love the other, or he will hold to one and despise the other. You cannot serve God and Mammon."

"Mammon," of course, refers to riches. You can't serve *both* God and money. Remember the couple I mentioned in chapter 5 who went to see the strategic planner? He asked them which word they wanted to put in the box: *Jesus* or *money*. They couldn't have both running their lives.

Neither can we. If money runs our lives, then our finances don't reflect a biblical view of success. If God runs our lives, then we'll look at money as a resource and a responsibility that God has entrusted to us.

Money is an important asset, though, and should be managed carefully. Here are two principles to help you manage yours with a godly perspective.

WEIGH ENJOYMENT OF POSSESSIONS AGAINST INVESTMENT IN OTHER PEOPLE

Right away you can see there are two extremes in the use of money. I've already mentioned this. On the one hand, we can lavish all of our money on ourselves, spending everything on our own comfort and convenience. On the other hand, we could liquidate all our assets and give everything away and live in poverty.

We'll always find people at either extreme. Obviously most will tend to prefer a lifestyle of luxury, but a few will feel called to poverty. For my own part, I think we need to keep both of these in tension. I believe we need to enjoy and thank God for what He's given us, but not overindulge ourselves and wrap ourselves in a lifestyle of comfort and convenience. Instead, we need to head in the other direction—investing in the lives of other people, actually spending and investing our resources to meet their needs. Our overall lifestyle should be marked by sacrifice and discipline. After all, that's the example Christ set for us (2 Corinthians 8:9):

> For you know the grace of our Lord Jesus Christ, that though He was rich, yet for your sake He became poor, that you through His poverty might become rich.

And this is the life to which He calls us (Matthew 16:24-26):

Then Jesus said to His disciples, "If any one wishes to come after Me, let him deny himself, and take up his cross, and follow Me. For whoever wishes to save his life shall lose it; but whoever loses his life for My sake shall find it. For what will a man be profited, if he gains the whole world, and forfeits his soul? Or what will a man give in exchange for his soul?"

What the balance looks like in your life between enjoyment versus investment is purely your decision. But, considering our culture, I would caution you that if most of your assets and most of your purchases are prestige items designed to enhance your image and impress other people, you should take a hard look at whether sacrifice and discipline characterize your life. Here's a practical idea to help you in this evaluation.

APPLY THE PRINCIPLE OF FUNCTIONAL ECONOMY TO YOUR PURCHASES

"Functional economy" means buying the least expensive thing that will get the job done over the long haul. Most purchases are intended to meet a need. That's fine. To make a wise choice, you should buy an item that gets the job done, but with an eye toward responsibility in the use of your money.

Oftentimes, of course, the least expensive thing that will get the job done is not the least expensive choice. Clothes are a good illustration of this. I can buy a suit very cheaply, but a cheap suit won't last long. So if I buy one, I'll likely have to replace it much sooner than if I'd paid more money for a nicer suit that will last much longer.

Functional economy realizes that usually we get what we pay for, so we must be careful in what we pay for. But it also tells us that we ought not to be buying things for prestige. Biblically, we should buy things for their function, not their image.

I realize that making an impression is important in our culture, and some purchases, like works of art, are more aesthetic than functional. But the point is that we should live responsibly and not bury ourselves under luxuries. Instead of spending all our money on ourselves, we need to be spending a good portion of it on others, to meet their needs.

Our money is a valuable resource for which we will give an account to God someday. Don't squander yours on yourself. Instead, heed the challenge of Paul in 1 Timothy 6:17-19:

> Instruct those who are rich in this present world not to be conceited or to fix their hope on the uncertainty of riches, but on God, who richly supplies us with all things to enjoy. Instruct them to do good, to be rich in good works, to be generous and ready to share, storing up for themselves the treasure of a good foundation for the future, so that they may take hold of that which is life indeed.

CHAPTER SEVENTEEN

Don't Stop Here!

One of the real dangers in writing a book like this is that it could just end up producing smarter sinners! After all, this is a book about beliefs. And as we all know, it's easy to know the right beliefs, yet not really believe them. It's easy to affirm biblical truth, yet live in total contradiction to it.

However, I'm assuming that if you've read this far, it's not out of sheer intellectual curiosity, nor is it because you plan to live in opposition to what God has said in His Word. Instead, I suspect that you want to adopt a biblical view of success and see it make a practical difference in our life. So the question is: How can you do that—where do you get started? Here are five practical steps you can take right away.

SET ONE GOAL IN EACH MAJOR AREA OF LIFE

True success means pursuing a measure of faithfulness in every area of your life, not just work. So devise a simple goal for each of the five major categories—

personal life, family, work, church, and community. What is one simple, practical, measurable, achievable step you can take in each of these areas? (See chapter 5, pages 76-81, for a review of this principle.)

SPEND TIME ALONE WITH GOD EACH DAY

In chapter 5 we described the need to cultivate a close, intimate relationship with Christ. This is a lifelong process, and there's no way to do it apart from spending some period of time with Him every day. I suggest feeding on short Scripture passages, examining them carefully to understand what they mean, what difference they make in your life, and what they tell you about God. I also recommend a concentrated time in prayer.

There's no need to be legalistic or neurotic about this daily discipline; obviously there will be days when you can't squeeze time in. But, as with any relationship with another person, you can't build intimacy with God unless you spend time with Him, just the two of you.

WRITE A CAREER MANIFESTO

In chapter 13, I encouraged you to write a one-page purpose statement of how you could display Christlikeness in your particular job situation. For many people, taking this step has proven to be a real breakthrough in making Christ relevant to their day-to-day experience.

TELL AT LEAST ONE OTHER PERSON ABOUT HOW YOU INTEND TO BE DIFFERENT

If you've been gripped by the concept of a biblical view of success, if you can see at least one way that it will make a difference in your life, then tell someone else about that! Nothing else will cement your conviction like explaining it to a friend or associate. I strongly encourage you to recruit several of your friend to a discussion group, using this book. This brings us to a final suggestion.

DON'T STOP HERE!

Keep going into the study guide that follows. There you'll find a series of questions and exercises to help you begin to weave the principles of this book into your attitudes and behavior. You can work your way through it on your own; or, better yet, team up with a group of your peers who also want to pursue true success.

I've watched hundreds of people just like you go through this process and seen it change their lives. It's not that there's any magic to the material; it's that they were *doing* something instead of *thinking* about doing something. If you want life-change, going through the exercises that follow is the place to get started.

So don't stop here! Turn the page and get started on a process that can translate truth into action. When you've completed that material, write and tell me about your experience, using the response guidelines in the back of the book. Bill and I and the rest of the team at CIM are praying for you, that as you follow through with this process you'll embrace a truly biblical outlook on your success and all the benefits it offers—the wonderful new freedoms, the power new values, and the dynamic new way of making decisions. Let us know how our prayers have been answered in *your* life, so that we can all rejoice in God together!

The next step is yours. I urge you to take it now!

Your Success Strategy: A Manual for Growth

The material that follows is a six-part manual to help you apply the principles in this book to your life. There's no question that while we retain very little of what we read, we retain nearly all of what we do. In the sessions that follow, you'll *do* far more than you'll read!

Here's how to gain the most from this material.

USE IT WITH A GROUP

We find that small discussion groups are an ideal way to apply biblical truth to life. That's why we've designed this for discussion, not just self-study. We strongly encourage you to interact with a group of your friends using this manual. To have an effective group, you'll need to do several things:

1. Limit the group's size to six or eight people. If you have nine or more, we recommend splitting into two groups.

2. Make sure each participant has a copy of this book.

3. Be clear as to the time and place for the discussion.

4. Clarify expectations before you begin. Everyone should agree on the purpose of the group and the level of commitment to it.

5. Set a termination date for the group, or at least for using this book. Don't ask people for open-ended commitments.

6. Appoint a discussion leader. This person is not a teacher, but someone who can facilitate a healthy group interaction.

7. Keep the discussion focused. The questions and material in this guide have been designed to help you think and talk about important issues. Don't get sidetracked. Encourage everyone to participate. This is a discussion, not a lecture or a platform for one person's point of view.

8. Come prepared to discuss. The preparation involved is minimal. Each session corresponds to sections of the book, so reading the material ahead of time will help. However, someone can easily participate in the discussion even if that person hasn't read the book.

9. We haven't left much space in this guide to write many notes, so you may find it helpful to record answers to some questions in a separate notebook or journal. This will prove especially helpful for the exercises that require extended responses and reflection.

10. Some of the questions in this guide ask for painfully honest disclosure. For example, the personal inventory in Session 3 asks you to tell about areas of your life where you feel you could be stronger. To make this kind of vulnerability possible and healthy, you must agree to maintain strict confidences, to avoid judgment, and to strive for honesty even when it's uncomfortable.

SUGGESTIONS FOR GROUP LEADERS

You have an important role to play in making this experience helpful for everyone. In any group situation, someone's got to get things rolling and keep things moving. That's your job! If you do it well, the other natural dynamics of the group process will take care of everything else.

1. Come prepared. At a minimum, this involves reading the book and previewing the particular session that your group will cover. Doing so will give you confidence and a sense of where things are headed during the discussion. Moreover, your preparation sets a vital example for the other participants. It shows them how seriously you take the group, and therefore, how seriously they should take it.

2. In preparation for Session 1, you'll need to select, from among the three stories in Chapter 2, the one that seems most relevant to your group.

3. Your goal is to keep a lively discussion going. You can do that by probing people's responses, asking for clarification, and raising thought-provoking questions. Of course, others in the group should be encouraged to do the same. Whatever you do, avoid "teaching" the content of the book.

4. Don't let someone dominate the group with his or her opinions or personality. Try to get each participant—especially shy or quiet ones—to say at least one or two things at each session.

5. Keep track of the time. Before the group meets, think through how much time should be allotted to each section of the session. That way you can keep things moving. We've designed each session to have resolution and completion, so if the last few questions or exercises

are not covered, people may feel frustrated. By the way, the ideal length of time for a discussion is an hour to an hour and fifteen minutes.

6. End the discussion on time. People have other responsibilities and commitments. If the session lasts too long, they may develop a negative attitude toward the group. By contrast, cutting off a lively interaction will bring everyone back with enthusiasm. Our rule is, "Leave them longing, not loathing!"

THIS GUIDE CAN BE USED FOR SELF-STUDY

Discussion groups won't work for everyone. That's okay. You can still enjoy valuable benefits from this guide even in self-study. Just make a couple of adjustments.

1. You'll have to be much more self-disciplined, because you won't have the built-in accountability of a group. We recommend that you determine a specific time and place to study. Then put that in your appointment book so you won't crowd it out with other commitments.

2. Since you won't have a group to discuss the material with, you'll spend a great deal of effort in personal reflection and thought. Writing (or taping) will replace discussing. However, you should seek opportunities to discuss your ideas with others—coworkers, your spouse, other Christians. These people will be invaluable in helping you gain perspective and offering you objective feedback, even though they will participate on an informal basis.

Session 1

In this session you'll evaluate some of our culture's perspectives on success.

Part One
SUGGESTED TIME: 25-30 MINUTES

On pages 13-14, I mention a newspaper feature written about my friend Peter. Review the description and then discuss the following questions.

1. Is Peter a success? Why or why not?

2. The article seems to suggest that Peter is a success. Do you think Peter feels this way? Why would he or wouldn't he?

3. What does it take for a person to succeed in our society?

4. Would you want what Peter has? Why or why not?

Part Two
SUGGESTED TIME: 20-30 MINUTES

In chapter 2, we said that our culture tends to measure success in terms of four criteria: money, professional recognition, power, and the four Cs—closet space, cars, clubs, and clothes.

5. Which of these are especially important among your friends and coworkers?

6. What additional items might you add to this list as being marks of success in our society?

7. How would someone in your occupation know if they were successful?

8. Why do you think success is so important in our culture?

Part Three
SUGGESTED TIME: 10 MINUTES

Read the following four quotes.

> I hunger for success. I thirst for happiness and peace of mind. Lest I act I will perish in a life of failure, misery, and sleepless nights. I will command, and I will obey my own command.
> Og Mandino,
> *The Greatest Salesman in the World*

Every human being who reaches the age of understanding of the purpose of money wishes for it.

Wishing will not bring riches. But desiring riches
with a state of mind that becomes an obsession,
then planning definite ways and means to acquire
riches, and backing those plans with persistence
which does not recognize failure, will bring
riches.

Napoleon Hill,
How to Think and Grow Rich

The simple ambition to live better is a potent factor in succeeding . . . what you have now has to
be intolerable compared to what you want. The
more you see the future in concrete terms of material gain, the easier it is to get there . . . we owe it
to ourselves to enjoy life.

Michael Korda,
Success!

It's o.k. to be greedy.
It's o.k. to be ambitious.
It's o.k. to look out for Number One.
It's o.k. to have a good time.
It's o.k. to be Machiavellian (if you can get away
with it).
It's o.k. to recognize that honesty is not always the
best policy (provided you don't go around saying
so).
It's o.k. to be a winner.
And, it's *always* o.k. to be rich.

A word of caution: People will tell you that success
can't buy happiness. This is true enough, but
success is the next best thing to happiness, and
if you can't be happy as a success, it's very

unlikely that you would find a deeper, truer happiness in failure.

>Michael Korda,
>*Success!*

Discussion Questions

9. What are some of the specific values revealed in these four quotes?

10. Do you think someone who adopted the values and ideas of these writers would succeed? Why or why not?

11. To what extent do you agree or disagree with the statements of these writers?

12. On a scale of 1 to 10 (with 10 being most important), how important is career success to you? Why?

Part Four
SUGGESTED TIME: 5 MINUTES

I want you to get the most from this book and the sessions that follow. But a lot depends on you and what you plan to gain from this experience. Reflect for a few moments on how you would complete the statement below, then write down your response.

As a result of going through this book and the exercises in this study guide, I'd like to see changes in my life such as . . .

On Your Own
1. Memorize Jeremiah 9:23-24: "Thus says the LORD, 'Let not a wise man boast of his wisdom, and let not the mighty man boast of his might, let not a rich man boast of his riches; but let him who boasts boast of this, that he understands and knows Me, that I am the LORD who exercises lovingkindness, justice, and righteousness on earth; for I delight in these things,' declares the LORD."

2. Ask three of your coworkers this question: How will you know when you've reached success in your life? Record their responses.

3. In a separate notebook, write a one-page essay entitled, "My Definition of Success." If you dislike writing, use a dictaphone, or explain to a friend what success would be like for you.

4. To prepare for session 2, carefully read chapter 3.

Session 2

*In this session you'll evaluate two views of
success that some Christians hold.*

Part One
SUGGESTED TIME: 30-40 MINUTES

Read the following testimonial and then discuss the
questions following it.

The Missionary's Testimony
Thank you for the opportunity to speak on the
issue of missions, and why I think every committed Christian should be involved in full-time service to God.

Let me share with you a little bit of my background. Prior to attending seminary, I was a businessman involved in the sale of drill presses.
These drill presses were used in some of the more
sophisticated machine shops.

During the early years of business, I realized
it took a lot of time to get the business going, and
that limited my involvement in church. But as
time went on, I found more and more of an inter-

est in serving God. As I became more heavily involved, I began to reflect on my life and what I was doing in my day-to-day work. I became gripped by the fact that my whole life was given to a business that puts holes in metal—holes that are later filled up with screws!

The Things That Last
While I was thinking about this, I began to think of the things that last for eternity. This was prompted by a sermon my pastor gave one day on the two things that last for eternity—the Word of God and the souls of men.

As I pondered the significance of these things, I began to think about how meaningless my life was, given to making holes in metal that will someday be filled up with screws. Not only did this occupation seem meaningless, but the thought dawned on me that someday the whole earth will be destroyed, as it says in 2 Peter, and all the elements of the earth will melt—if it doesn't rust before then! The utter futility of my life as a businessman led me to start considering the ministry. I wanted to invest my life in things that will really last.

As I thought of this, I began to think about some of the frustrations I felt as a "part-time" servant of God. I was only able to attend church and be involved in the program on Wednesday nights, Sunday mornings, and Sunday nights. I realized that I was not only part-time, but I was also serving God only in my tired hours. And I felt He was worthy of something much more.

A Career Change

This led me to a very important decision concerning my career. Was I going to have a life given principally to something as futile as putting holes in metal, or to something that would really count? I began to consider what business is all about, and I realized that my whole motive for being in business was self-centered. I was principally in it to provide an income for myself and all the comforts I and my family wanted. Ultimately, I realized that my orientation was one of greed. I was just in it for myself.

Furthermore, I saw that I lived in a business culture dominated by self-centered and greedy thinking. And I knew that I could not continue to be around it without picking up the same values that that culture had. Self-centered values oppose every line of the Bible. I knew I wanted to be different and to live a different lifestyle.

Well, as if these things had not been enough to convince me, the final thing that struck me was a challenge I heard from a prominent Christian leader. He told me that as a minister of the gospel, I had the highest calling on the face of the earth!

As I thought about this, I could see why he would say that. Without question, the program of God in the world today is to save sinners and to sanctify saints. Drilling holes in metal is far removed from that work. In fact, if I wanted to be on the front line as a participant in God's work, and not just a spectator, I needed to give my life work to the things that really count.

Because of these reasons, I chose to go into full-time work for God.

A Challenge
Today I would challenge you to do the same. Sometimes I think that the ministry is one of the ways God has of filtering out uncommitted people. It's like Jesus told the rich, young ruler: "Sell all and follow Me." I realize that some must stay behind and make enough money to support the full-time people. And I'm grateful for them. But the fact remains, full-time servants are on the cutting edge of God's work!

Well, what about you? *You* don't have to be addicted to mediocrity! *You* don't have to live a half-hearted commitment to Christ! Jesus said in John 6:27, "Do not work for the food which perishes, but for the food which endures to eternal life." This is our Savior's exhortation to make our lives count! In light of this admonition, I challenge you to surrender yourself to a full-time life of service and ministry.[1]

1. Based on the comments he makes, describe how this missionary views everyday work, e.g., his former work as a salesman of drill presses.

2. Have you ever heard similar remarks made by someone in "full-time" Christian ministry? How did that experience make you feel about your "secular" job?

3. Ecclesiastes 5:18-19 calls work a gift from God: "Here is what I have seen to be good and fitting: to eat, to drink and enjoy oneself in all one's labor in which he toils under the sun during the few years of his life which God has given him: for this is his reward. Furthermore, as for every man to whom God has given

riches and wealth, He has also empowered him to eat from them and to receive his reward and rejoice in his labor; this is the gift of God."

Do you think that if this missionary had seen his work in sales as a gift from God, it could have made a difference in how he approached his job? How?

4. The missionary implies that only Christians in "full-time" ministry can "succeed" before God. How does that idea compare to the teaching of Ephesians 6:7-8, which is addressed to common slaves?

Part Two
SUGGESTED TIME: 25-30 MINUTES

"If Christians are poor and miserable, who would want to be one?" I believe that God made the diamonds for His children and not for Satan's. Psalm 23 says, "I will dwell in the house of the Lord forever." He has the facilities of the universe at His disposal, so I believe He is going to build quite a house. I can't believe He wants me or any of His children to live in a chicken shack between here and there.

Zig Ziglar,
Confessions of a Happy Christian

5. What values are promoted in the above quote? (Compare it with Jeremiah 9:23-24.)

6. a. Many of the early Christians at Corinth were apparently poor and miserable, both materially and spiritually. What does Paul say to these people in 1 Corinthians 1:26-31?

b. How might this New Testament passage contradict the Ziglar quote?

7. What kinds of behavior could one justify with the idea that "God made the diamonds for His children"?

8. What does the last sentence of the quote say to poor Christians who actually *do* live in virtual chicken shacks—or worse?

Part Three
SUGGESTED TIME: 20 MINUTES

If you *want* financial strength and security, it is available if you will follow God's teachings. . . . All I'm suggesting is that if you are broke, you shouldn't blame God for your problem because He wrote the book on how to prosper. Question: Do you believe the Book? Jesus spoke to us very clearly on this point: "Ye have not because ye ask not."

Zig Ziglar,
Confessions of a Happy Christian

9. a. The quote of Ziglar implies that the Bible teaches a path to material prosperity, that godliness leads to financial gain. What does Paul say about this in 1 Timothy 6:3-10?

b. According to Paul, which desires should we pursue, and which should we avoid? (See verses 17-19.)

10. James (not Jesus) wrote that "ye have not, because ye ask not" (James 4:2, KJV). However, read the entire context of the verse, James 4:1-4.

a. James is discussing conflicts and fights among believers. What does he say is the root cause of such problems?

b. What is the answer to these problems? (See verses 7-10.)

c. How does the attitude that James promotes compare with the attitudes promoted by prosperity theology?

On Your Own

1. Review your memorization of Jeremiah 9:23-24.

2. Memorize Colossians 3:17: "And whatever you do in word or deed, do all in the name of the Lord Jesus, giving thanks through Him to God the Father."

3. Obtain a copy of our book *Your Work Matters to God*, and begin reading it to consider what the Bible teaches about everyday work.

4. If you know someone who seems to hold to a Prosperity Theology, ask him why he believes as he does. Perhaps you can discuss together the questions in part two of this session.

5. In preparation for session 3, carefully read chapters 4 and 5, about the Bible's teaching on success.

NOTE   1. Doug Sherman and William Hendricks, *Your Work Matters to God* (Colorado Springs, Colo.: NavPress, 1987), pages 43-45.

Session 3

*In this session you'll evaluate some of the
Bible's teaching on success.*

Part One
SUGGESTED TIME: 20-25 MINUTES

In chapter 4 I discuss the parable of the talents, and use it
to illustrate some key features of a biblical view of
success. Here is the parable in its complete form. Read it
through carefully, two or three times, and then answer
the questions that follow.

"For it is just like a man about to go on a journey,
who called his own slaves, and entrusted his possessions to them.

"And to one he gave five talents, to another,
two, and to another, one, each according to his
own ability; and he went on his journey.

"Immediately the one who had received the
five talents went and traded with them, and
gained five more talents.

"In the same manner the one who had received the two talents gained two more.

"But he who received the one talent went away and dug in the ground, and hid his master's money.

"Now after a long time the master of those slaves came and settled accounts with them.

"And the one who had received the five talents came up and brought five more talents, saying, 'Master, you entrusted five talents to me; see, I have gained five more talents.'

"His master said to him, 'Well done, good and faithful slave; you were faithful with a few things, I will put you in charge of many things, enter into the joy of your master.'

"The one also who had received the two talents came up and said, 'Master, you entrusted to me two talents; see, I have gained two more talents.'

"His master said to him, 'Well done, good and faithful slave; you were faithful with a few things, I will put you in charge of many things; enter into the joy of your master.'

"And the one also who had received the one talent came up and said, 'Master, I knew you to be a hard man, reaping where you did not sow, and gathering where you scattered no seed.

'And I was afraid, and went away and hid your talent in the ground; see, you have what is yours.'

"But his master answered and said to him, 'You wicked, lazy slave, you knew that I reap where I did not sow, and gather where I scattered no seed.

'Then you ought to have put my money in the bank, and on my arrival I would have received my money back with interest.

'Therefore take away the talent from him, and give it to the one who has the ten talents.'

"For to everyone who has shall more be given, and he shall have an abundance; but from the one who does not have, even what he does have shall be taken away.

"And cast out the worthless slave into the outer darkness; in that place there shall be weeping and gnashing of teeth." (Matthew 25:14-30)

1. What were the differences between the third slave and his two associates?

2. What were the criteria by which the master evaluated his servants?

3. What did the first and second slaves receive as rewards from the master, and why did they receive rewards?

4. Why did the third slave get punished so severely? (What was his crime?)

5. We argue that true success means faithfully pleasing God with the resources and responsibilities He's given us. As you consider your own life and work, and the resources and responsibilities God has entrusted to you, which of the three slaves do you feel you are most like? Why?

Part Two
SUGGESTED TIME: 20-25 MINUTES

The case study of John follows. John is a young lawyer and father. Read this case study and answer the questions following it.

John

John is a young lawyer who aspires to become a partner in his law firm. He loves his work—so much so that he puts in many late nights, and even works two or three weekends a month to demonstrate his loyalty and support for the firm.

John's hard work, perseverance, and intelligence may soon pay off. His boss has given indications that John is being considered for partnership in the organization. This would add substantially to John's professional stature as well as to his income.

However, for some time John has sensed that his life may be somewhat out of balance. He feels nagging guilt over being away from his wife and three children so much. His wife is terribly proud of his achievements, but recently she's complained that he is becoming a stranger to her.

Meanwhile, John's children are growing up fast! His son is almost a teenager already. John worries because the boy seems so shy and insecure around his peers. And his two young daughters seem to quarrel constantly. Their behavior irritates him when he comes home, tired and just wanting a quiet rest. He finds himself looking for excuses to stay at the office until after their bedtime.

In his few private moments, John finds that his relationship with Christ is superficial. He rarely has time to read his Bible, and prays only at family meals or at church. On the other hand, he contributes what he feels is a sizable amount to his church and to a local youth home. His pastor has even thanked him on occasion for his support and once told him, "We rely on you, John!"

All in all, John feels that he is doing what it takes to succeed in life. He deals with his nagging doubts about his family life by reasoning: "Once I make partnership, I'll be able to spend more time with my family. We'll be able to afford all kinds of fun activities together!"

6. Do you think John is typical of many workers who are young and want to succeed? Explain your reasoning.

7. John is a religious person. To what extent do you think his outlook on life reflects a biblical view of success?

8. Why do you think regular Bible reading is not included in John's schedule?

9. What suggestions would you make that might help John do a better job of faithfully pleasing God with the resources and responsibilities He's given him?

Part Three
SUGGESTED TIME: 15-20 MINUTES

In chapter 5 I suggest three important steps that a person must take if he ever hopes to enjoy true success:

•Cultivate a close, intimate relationship with Christ.

•Learn God's assignments for your life.
•Commit yourself to living with a godly view of success.

Answer the following questions:

10. Which *one* of the following words *best* describes the relationship you have with Jesus right now?

Right now, Jesus seems like a . . .
•power or force
•best friend
•stranger
•lover
•boss
•just a friend
•idea or abstraction
•father
•acquaintance
•judge
•enemy
•other (name it)

11. a. Which one of the words above best describes what you'd most like your relationship with Jesus to become?

b. How might you go about cultivating that kind of relationship?

12. For each of the areas in the chart on the following page, list two ways in which you believe you are carrying out God's assignments for your life, and two ways you feel you need to improve. An example is given.

Area	I'm doing well in . . .	I could stand to improve in . . .
Personal Life	*Reading my Bible.*	*The habit I have of gossiping.*
Personal Life		
Family		
Work		
Church		
Community		

13. Committing yourself to living with a godly view of success involves a commitment to:
    - Christ's lordship,
    - Life-change,
    - Ethical purity,
    - Godly decision-making,
    - Trusting God for outcome.

    For each of these five areas, determine one way in which you could start demonstrating your commitment to a godly view of success. An example is given.

    Example: Christ's lordship—As I arrive at work, I will pause to pray, "Lord, I come here as Your employee. Use my work to meet the needs of people. Use my life to impact others. Because my work really matters to

*You, I want to do it in a way that pleases You. Help me
do that today."*

On Your Own

1. Review your memorization of Jeremiah 9:23-24 and
   Colossians 3:17.

2. Memorize Matthew 16:24-26: "Then Jesus said to His
   disciples, 'If anyone wishes to come after Me, let him
   deny himself, and take up his cross, and follow Me.
   For whoever wishes to save his life shall lose it; but
   whoever loses his life for My sake shall find it. For
   what will a man be profited, if he gains the whole
   world, and forfeits his soul? Or what will a man give
   in exchange for his soul?'"

3. Earlier, I spelled out five areas that are involved in
   committing yourself to a godly view of success.
   Discuss the five aspects that this commitment involves with your spouse or someone who knows you
   well.

   What would your life look like if you made this
   five-fold commitment?

4. In preparation for session 4, carefully read chapters
   6-9 about the new freedoms that come from a biblical
   view of success.

Session 4

*In this session you'll examine
the new freedoms that come from a biblical
view of success.*

Part One

SUGGESTED TIME: 15 MINUTES

True success involves freedom from anxiety about career success—to an enjoyment of work and leisure.

> It is good and proper for a man to eat and drink, and to find satisfaction in his toilsome labor under the sun during the few days of life God has given him—for this is his lot. Moreover, when God gives any man wealth and possessions, and enables him to enjoy them, to accept his lot and be happy in his work—this is a gift of God. (Ecclesiastes 54:18-19, NIV)

1. Why do you think so many people feel anxiety about career success?

2. Ecclesiastes teaches that work and its rewards are good and proper—in fact, they are a *gift* from God.

a. How would your attitude toward your job change if you saw it as a gift from God?

b. What would be your attitude toward success?

3. What would it take for *you* to be free from anxiety about career success?

Part Two
SUGGESTED TIME: 15-20 MINUTES

True success involves freedom from frantic busyness and overwork—to a balanced lifestyle.

Review the case history of John in session 3 (pages 200-201). Notice that John's life is out of balance, fraught with guilt and tension.

4. John is in a position of high stress, facing demands from work and other areas of life, but meeting few of them well. Why do you think he has landed in this cycle of frantic busyness and overwork?

5. a. What practical, biblical steps would you recommend to John to bring his life into balance?

b. Which of these suggestions could you use yourself?

Part Three
SUGGESTED TIME: 15-20 MINUTES

True success involves freedom from comparing ourselves to others—to a concern for others.

6. Describe someone you know who has more wealth, more power, or more success than you.

7. Now, describe someone you know who has less wealth, power, or success than you.

8. How would our culture rank you and the two people you described?

9. How would a biblical view of success affect how you think about and behave toward both of these individuals?

10. How would a biblical view of success affect how you think about your own material possessions?

Part Four
SUGGESTED TIME: 10-15 MINUTES

True success involves freedom from trying to be perfect—to accepting ourselves the way we are.

To succeed, it is necessary to accept the world as it is and rise above it. . . .

We must learn . . . to develop that inner spark that demands the highest of us, that tells every one of us that it is better to succeed [than] to fail, that we are responsible for using our strengths and resources to the utmost, and that life on any other terms is a waste. A society which is built around the notion of success for the individual may be cruel, as ours often is, but it is at least free, in the sense that we are responsible for ourselves and our own choices, for everyone has the right and the need to succeed.

Michael Korda,
Success!

11. What would it take for you to rise above the world?

12. Do you think a person who followed Korda's suggestions would be truly free? Why or why not?

13. Read Psalm 139:13-16. This passage has profound implications for the worth and dignity of an individual. How does this biblical view of worth contrast with the view promoted by Korda?

On Your Own
1. Review your memorization of Jeremiah 9:23-24, Colossians 3:17, and Matthew 16:24-26.

2. Memorize Galatians 5:1,13: "It was for freedom that Christ set us free; therefore keep standing firm and do not be subject again to a yoke of slavery. . . . For you were called to freedom, brethren; only do not turn your freedom into an opportunity for the flesh, but through love serve one another."

3. Select one of the four freedoms we've looked at and list three practical ways you could begin practicing that freedom. An example is given here.

Example: Freedom from frantic busyness and overwork—to a balanced lifestyle.
•I could set a come-home time so that I leave work in time to be home with my family.

•I could arrange each Sunday evening to review my weekly schedule with my spouse so that we think through our lives together.
•I could set one specific, measurable, achievable goal in each of five areas—personal life, family, work, church, and community.

4. Obtain a copy of our book *How to Balance Competing Time Demands* as a way to get started toward a fully-orbed, biblical lifestyle.

5. In preparation for session 5, carefully read chapters 10-13 about the new values that a biblical view of success fosters.

Session 5

*In this session you'll examine the new values
that a biblical view of success promotes.*

A biblical view of success offers us new values. The
exercises that follow will help you examine some of these
new values.

But first, consider this passage:

Who is wise and understanding among you? Let
him show it by his good life, by deeds done in the
humility that comes from wisdom. But if you har-
bor bitter envy and selfish ambition in your
hearts, do not boast about it or deny the truth.
Such "wisdom" does not come down from heaven
but is earthly, unspiritual, of the devil. For where
you have envy and selfish ambition, there you find
disorder and every evil practice.

But the wisdom that comes from heaven is
first of all pure; then peace-loving, considerate,
submissive, full of mercy and good fruit, impar-
tial and sincere. Peacemakers who sow in peace
raise a harvest of righteousness. (James 3:13-18,
NIV)

James says there are two kinds of wisdom—the wisdom from "above" and the wisdom from "below." The key to appreciating James's point is to understand that in the Bible, *wisdom* means "the skill of living."

James is saying that you can bring one of two sets of skills to how you live your life: You can employ the skills that accomplish a selfish, ambitious agenda; or you can employ the skills that accomplish God's agenda—peace, love, consideration, mercy, etc.

Which set of skills you employ says everything about your *values*. People who pursue God's view of success embrace entirely new values, and therefore employ a new set of skills.

Just to remind yourself of the skills that accomplish a selfish, ambition-driven agenda, go back and re-read Michael Korda's hard-boiled list of success strategies on page 187. As you review this list, think about the values he is promoting.

With these two perspectives in mind—the wisdom of God versus the wisdom of the world—evaluate the following four situations.

Part One
SUGGESTED TIME: 10-15 MINUTES

True success involves a nonchalance about professional recognition but a deep concern about integrity.

The owner of a rather large retail chain was recently thinking and praying about his life, his career, his company, and his walk with God. It occurred to him that one inconsistency in his professional life was that, while he advocated moral purity as a nonnegotiable of his faith, his stores were selling softcore pornographic magazines at the checkout counter. So he told one of his vice presidents to remove the magazines.

"But sir!" the executive protested. "We make several *million* dollars a year off these products!"

"Several million, eh?" the boss responded. "Let me think about it."

The next day he returned from a sleepless night and called the executive into his office. "Get rid of the magazines!" he ordered. "No price is too great to pay to do what is right."

1. In this true story, a man obviously acted according to the wisdom from above.

   a. What was "wise" about his choice?

   b. What did this costly decision reveal about his values?

2. a. The record indicates that this man's company actually *increased* its revenues after his decision, and the company was later sold at a substantial profit. But suppose that the company had gone bust after his decision—in fact, that this choice actually led to its downfall. Would you still say that he made the right choice? Why?

   b. What determines whether a choice is the right choice?

3. Have you ever been in a similar situation, or are you in one right now? How does it challenge your values?

Part Two
SUGGESTED TIME: 15-20 MINUTES

True success involves a nonchalance about ladders and titles but a deep concern with character growth.

Ellen and Sharon sat talking over lunch one day. Ellen was with a small advertising firm. She had achieved modest success in her career, though this was not a major goal for her. Rather, she placed priority on balancing her time between work and other commitments—her husband and children, her church, her neighbors, etc. Furthermore, her personal character and its growth meant everything to her, certainly more than career advancement.

By contrast, Sharon was an entrepreneur whose business smarts had catapulted her to prominence in the community. Her walls were covered with plaques, letters of commendation, and pictures of her shaking hands with various political and civic leaders.

Reflecting on her friend's status and prosperity, Ellen remarked, "It must be very gratifying to you to enjoy such a place of influence and importance in this town."

"I'll tell you what," Sharon shot back. "I'd give it all up in a *minute* to have the quality of life and faith that you have!"

4. Sharon was impressed with Ellen, even though Ellen's career seemed fairly unimpressive. Why? (What did Sharon see in Ellen?)

5. Why would Sharon even consider giving up her obviously successful position?

6. a. What character traits do the two kinds of wisdom mentioned in James 3 produce?

   b. Which of these traits would you like to see more of in your own life?

   c. Which would you like to see less of?

Part Three
SUGGESTED TIME: 15-20 MINUTES

True success involves a nonchalance about financial status but a deep concern about relationships.

Imagine that your boss is a real jerk! Thoughtless, impatient, gutter-mouthed, and ambitious, he runs your company with reckless ambition, risking catastrophe with every new decision.

On payday you pick up your check and discover that you've received a salary increase of *half* what was promised you!

As you head for your car, an associate suddenly says, "Boy, did you hear about the boss! Somebody told me his doctor called him this afternoon and says he's got diabetes. That ought to slow him down!"

7. a. Given Michael Korda's success strategy advice, what strategic advantages could you take of this situation?

   b. What would be the benefits to you?

8. a. James and other New Testament writers place a premium on quality relationships. How might a

Christian who valued such relationships respond to the above situation?

b. What are some of the issues that ought to be considered?

9. a. What relationships in your own life are under stress right now because of tensions between career success and the needs of people?

b. What action could you take to show compassion and concern?

Part Four
SUGGESTED TIME: 15 MINUTES

True success involves a nonchalance about the approval of others but a deep concern with serving God at work.

You and Elizabeth are two lawyers in a fairly prestigious law firm. Having attended law school together, you are both excited about your potential as professional women in what has been a traditionally male-dominated field. In fact, you are in competition with each other to be named the firm's first female partner.

Frankly, you suspect that Elizabeth will win that honor. After all, she has a mind like a steel trap, argues her cases with clarity and style, and most importantly, exhibits superior management skills. You, on the other hand, excel in devising legal strategy and researching precedent. But you definitely dislike overseeing the work of others, choosing to work independently on projects.

One day, the senior partners call you into their conference room. "Congratulations!" they gush. "We'd like to offer you a partnership in the firm."

You express gratitude and so forth, and then the discussion rolls around to why they selected you. "We need a strategist right now," one of them explains. "That's why we selected you over Elizabeth. We need her to be on the firing line. You'll be back here, thinking through our moves, advising on some of our bigger cases. And, oh yeah, you'll be supervising the staff quite a bit. That's an area where we've had problems lately. What do you say?"

10. This opportunity offers both great advantages and great dangers. What are some of each?

11. Suppose your response to the offer were, "I appreciate this offer, gentlemen. But based on the nature of your needs right now, I think you might want to reconsider Elizabeth. After all, if you need a manager for the staff, she's much better qualified for that."

   a. Would you be a fool to point this out? Why?

   b. What would such a statement reveal about your values?

12. Colossians 3:23 speaks of working "heartily, as for the Lord rather than for men." How might a concern for working "as for the Lord" affect your response to this outstanding opportunity?

On Your Own
   1. Review your memorization of Jeremiah 9:23-24; Colossians 3:17; Matthew 16:24-26; and Galatians 5:1,13.

2. Memorize Psalm 19:7-11: "The law of the LORD is perfect, restoring the soul; the testimony of the LORD is sure, making wise the simple. The precepts of the LORD are right, rejoicing the heart; the commandment of the LORD is pure, enlightening the eyes. The fear of the LORD is clean, enduring forever; the judgments of the LORD are true; they are righteous altogether. They are more desirable than gold, yes, than much fine gold; sweeter also than honey and the drippings of the honeycomb. Moreover, by them, Thy servant is warned; in keeping them there is great reward."

3. Select one of the four new values we've looked at and list three practical steps you could take to build that value into your life.

Example: A nonchalance about ladders and titles but a deep concern about character growth.
•My character needs to change in the area of gossiping. The next time I'm tempted to gossip, I'm going to steer the conversation in a more positive direction.
•My character needs to change in the area of keeping my word. Next time I make a commitment, I'm going to ask someone to hold me accountable to follow through.
•My character needs to change in the area of reporting my travel expenses to the company accurately and honestly. On my next trip, I'm going to carry a small notebook and keep closer tabs on my spending.

4. Begin reading one verse or one chapter from the book of Proverbs each day, in order to fill your mind and conscience with godly wisdom and values.

5. On pages 149-150, I discuss the usefulness of writing a "career manifesto" as a way to get started on applying biblical values to your work. Write such a statement of purpose about your job, using the instructions from chapter 13.

6. In preparation for session 6, carefully read chapters 14-16 about the way a biblical view of success affects one's decision making.

Session 6

In this session you'll examine how a biblical view of success affects your decisions in three areas—your integrity, schedule, and money. You'll also evaluate what you've learned by going through this book.

Part One
SUGGESTED TIME: 15-20 MINUTES

1. Describe a situation you are facing right now where your integrity is at stake.

2. a. If it's a question of honesty or dishonesty, what would telling the truth cost you?

   b. Are you willing to pay that price to maintain your integrity?

3. a. If it's a question of violating your conscience, what is it in the situation to which you object?

   b. What biblical principles might be involved?

   c. Are you willing to suffer any potential consequences to maintain your integrity?

4. a. If it's a matter of keeping your word, to what have you committed yourself?

   b. What will following through on your commitment mean for you?

   c. Are you prepared to do that?

Part Two
SUGGESTED TIME: 10-15 MINUTES

Take the following inventory by circling "yes" or "no" in response to each question. Don't spend much time trying to decide between the two. Usually, the first answer that comes to your mind is the most accurate.

Personal Life
1. Do you have a daily time of reading the Bible? Yes No
2. Have you read completely through the Bible? Yes No
3. Do you have a regular Bible study or discipleship group with whom you meet? Yes No
4. Do you have a daily time of prayer? Yes No
   When and for how long? _____
5. Do you have a prayer plan to pray for people? Yes No
6. Do you regularly meet with a friend socially? Yes No
7. Do you plan regular periods of rest and recreation on a weekly, monthly, and annual basis? Yes No
8. Do you consider yourself overweight? Yes No

9. Do you feel you should get more
exercise?   Yes   No

10. Do you regularly discuss your needs
and problems, thoughts and feelings
with your spouse and/or a close friend?   Yes   No

Family

1. Do you and your spouse "date"
regularly?   Yes   No

2. Do you regularly have family
devotions?   Yes   No

3. Do you regularly take time to talk with
your spouse about anything that
matters to either of you?   Yes   No

4. Do you regularly spend individual time
with each of your children, giving
them focused attention?   Yes   No
When and how long? _____

5. Would your family rate you as physi-
cally affectionate?   Yes   No

6. Does your family plan family fun and
togetherness each week?   Yes   No

7. Wives, would your husband say you
follow his leadership?   Yes   No

8. Husbands, would your wife say you are
a good leader?   Yes   No

9. If your parents are still living, do you
call or visit them regularly to see what
their needs are?   Yes   No

10. Do you have a budget to control your
family finances?   Yes   No
Where is it? _____

11. Do you and your spouse have a weekly
time of planning?   Yes   No

Work

1. Do you regularly plan out your day and set priorities?   Yes   No
2. Do you routinely pray for coworkers?   Yes   No
   When? _____
3. Could you give a clear presentation of the gospel to a nonChristian coworker?   Yes   No
4. Can you point to one area of your job in which you've improved in the past year?   Yes   No
   What is it? _____
5. Do you stay current with changes and developments in your profession?   Yes   No
6. Is there any area of ethical compromise in your work?   Yes   No
   What is it? _____
7. Are you clear on how your job helps others?   Yes   No
8. Do you tend to work too many hours?   Yes   No
9. Do you worry excessively about your work?   Yes   No
10. Do you find that problems at your work cause significant frustration and anger when you come home?   Yes   No

Church

1. Do you know what your spiritual gift is?   Yes   No
2. Do you talk with and affirm your pastor?   Yes   No
3. Do you have a regular program of giving to those who proclaim the gospel?   Yes   No
4. Do you have regular fellowship with others who will challenge you

spiritually?   Yes   No
5. Do you regularly call or write other
   Christians to thank them for something
   they've done or to encourage them in
   their faith?   Yes   No
6. Do you routinely pray for other Chris-
   tians?   Yes   No
   When and for how long? _____
7. Do you ever practice hospitality to
   Christians in need?   Yes   No
8. Do you have anyone who holds you
   accountable to reach personal goals?   Yes   No
9. Do you have any direct contact with
   missionaries?   Yes   No
   Who? _____
10. Are you involved in any form of
    financial assistance to those in need?   Yes   No

Community

1. Do you regularly meet socially with
   nonChristians?   Yes   No
2. Do you have any close nonChristian
   friends?   Yes   No
3. Do nonChristians feel comfortable
   around you?   Yes   No
4. Do you know your neighbors?   Yes   No
5. Can you give a clear, concise presen-
   tation of the gospel?   Yes   No
6. Do you regularly pray for government
   leaders and other officials?   Yes   No
7. Are you involved in any community
   service projects?   Yes   No
   Which ones? _____
8. Are you giving money to feed the poor? Yes   No

9. Are you aware of the political issues in
   your area?   Yes   No
10. Have you shared the gospel with some-
    one in the last six months?   Yes   No
    To whom? _____

Look back over your responses in the inventory. List
below some areas of strength and some areas where
you need to grow stronger.

a. Areas of strength:

b. Areas needing growth:

Part Three
SUGGESTED TIME: 10 MINUTES

Let your character be free from the love of money,
being content with what you have; for He Himself
has said, "I will never desert you, nor will I ever
forsake you." (Hebrews 13:5)

5. Describe your attitude toward your present lifestyle
   and material possessions.

6. Do you rest in the conviction that God intends to meet
   your needs? Why or why not?

7. What one step do you think you need to take right away in the way you handle your money?

Part Four
SUGGESTED TIME: 10 MINUTES

You would be wise to complete the evaluation form on page 227 as a way of analyzing what you've gained from this book and these sessions. Then discuss the following questions with your group.

8. What was the best thing about this group experience?

9. What progress have we actually made toward living with a biblical view of success?

10. What one, specific way would you especially like to change in the coming months?

11. Is a discussion group like we've had something we'd like to continue in the future? If so, what practical issues or topics would be helpful to study together?

Part Five
SUGGESTED TIME: 5 MINUTES

Conclude the time with prayer:
•Thank God for the specific things you've learned and the ways He's already helped you grow.
•Ask God to give each group member strength, courage, and discipline to follow through with the goals and commitments each one has made.

On Your Own

1. Review your memorization of Jeremiah 9:23-24; Colossians 3:17; Matthew 16:24-26; Galatians 5:1,13; and Psalm 19:7-11.

2. Memorize Psalm 37:3-5: "Trust in the LORD, and do good; dwell in the land and cultivate faithfulness. Delight yourself in the LORD; and He will give you the desires of your heart. Commit your way to the LORD, trust also in Him, and He will do it."

3. Review your responses to parts 1, 2, and 3 of this session, preferably with your spouse. What specific, measurable, and achievable steps will you take right away in light of your discussion?

4. If you have not done so, complete the evaluation form on page 227.

5. Evaluate the value of this book and what you've gained from it with someone who knows you well, such as your spouse or a close friend.

Note: Be sure to mail your response to me, using the guidelines at the back of the book (see page 228). I want to know how this book has been helpful to you, as well as ways I can improve the materials to be even more helpful.

EVALUATION
FORM

If you've read this book and worked through all of the exercises in the six sessions in the study guide, you've done a lot of constructive work toward developing a biblical view of success. Now complete the job by evaluating your experience.

1. What percentage of the exercises and questions did you complete?

2. If you were part of a discussion group, how many of the group meetings did you participate in?

3. To what extent do you think this experience will make a difference in your life and how you pursue success?

1	2	3	4	5
No Difference			Major Difference	

4. Look back at your response to the question asked in part four of session 1 (page 188). You hoped to gain something from this experience. Did you?

5. Describe how this experience could have been more helpful.

We Want to Hear from You!

We would like to know how this material has affected your life, and how we can improve our resources to be more helpful. Please complete the two statements that follow and send your responses to:

Doug Sherman
Career Impact Ministries
P.O. Box 14115
Ben Franklin Station
Washington, DC 20044-4115

Include your name and address on the page with your responses.

As a result of your book, *How to Succeed Where It Really Counts*, I've changed my life in the following way:

One way this book could have been more helpful to me is: